I CAN'T JUST WRITE A BOOK

I Can't Just Write a Book

CATHY VONK

Epigraph Books
Rhinebeck, New York

Paperback ISBN 978-1-954744-02-8
eBook ISBN 978-1-954744-03-5

Library of Congress Control Number 2021902422

Book design by Colin Rolfe

Epigraph Books
22 East Market Street, Suite 304
Rhinebeck, NY 12572
(845) 876-4861
epigraphps.com

CHAPTER 1

Mom

"**S**o then my mom's like, 'You just need to write the book, Cathy.' Yeah, ok. Like I have time to write a book!"

I stared out the window at the warmish fall sunshine as my mommy-mobile glided down the Garden State Parkway, musing aloud for the 18 millionth time about why I can never, and will never, be able to pursue my career dreams.

My husband put the truck in cruise control and patiently listened for the 18 millionth time.

"I mean, I couldn't even finish the application for the freelance position, let alone actually GET the job and DO the writing."

"I can help you find the time to-"

"I couldn't even have a 5-minute phone conference with my boss yesterday! Vince actually walked into the dining room, WHILE I was on the phone, bleeding all over the carpet. While Grace sat at the table next to me, sobbing because she wiped peanut butter all over her Letter N project. They were fine all morning. Totally fine. I tell them I need a few minutes? BOOM. Blood, sweat, tears and Skippy Naturals, EVERYWHERE. Write a book. Ok, Mom."

"Well, maybe the freelance job would be a good idea to start-"

"And I honestly don't know if the freelance job is for me. I want to write- believe me. But I'm not sure researching 5 pieces per week and penning blogs about shipping containers and different types of investment strategies is really the soul-fulfilling stuff I've been dreaming about, you know?"

"Yeah, I can see that-"

"But honestly, you know, can beggars be choosers? Or am I supposed to hold out for my dream job that might never materialize? Maybe it's a foot in the door? Maybe I should just call them and ask what they think? Can you even call a company you've just applied to and ask them what they think you should be doing?"

"I don't think it would hurt-"

"Write a book. I mean come on. Where does she think I have the time to write a book?! She's insane."

So, to summarize:

1. My husband is the most patient, attentive listener I've ever met
2. My children (like most children) are wired to self-destruct whenever I need time to myself
3. I have no time to write a book
4. My mother is insane

I sighed dramatically, as any self-deprecating creative type worth her salt would do, and looked out the window again. It was a beautiful fall morning. There was no traffic. We were headed out for a day of vegan pizza (we have all the allergies), zoo animals, dinner at whatever fun bistro we could find, and window-shopping in a historical town (cobblestones and all). Our two children were cozy in their booster seats; chatting and giggling with each other; munching on snacks; and talking about pizza toppings and their fervent hope of seeing a giraffe. My high school sweetheart-turned-husband was very respectfully waiting for the next leg of my panic-induced rant as he played with the radio.

This life of mine, it's a good one. It's one that I once only dreamed about. And it's one that I made possible by stepping away from a career I never really wanted so that my husband could chase his dreams.

And that bugs me.

It bugs me when people proclaim (over and over again), "You're so lucky to have Pat. He's so smart and successful," or, even better, "You don't need a career; you're so lucky you have someone to take care of you!"

It bugs me when, if asked what their parents do, my kids excitedly talk about how smart and amazing their dad is, and their mom? "She sits in an office and shops online." HR, if you're reading this, it was one time, we were out of protein bars, and it was a slow day.

I just feel so...stuck. I constantly find myself looking at my friends and feeling very...less than.

Some of them put their careers on hold to take on the kick-ass role of SAHM. These women are insanely amazing. I am in total awe of them. Honestly, they should lead the country- anyone who can run on a bottle of seltzer, cold coffee, and leftover Spongebob mac and cheese for days at a time while still successfully raising tiny humans and keeping the house looking livable? They have my vote.

Some of them are juggling their careers with the momming- one of them is juggling her career; raising not one, not two, but three children; and completing a Master's Degree. One of them is a teacher during a pandemic, which takes the cake right there, but she's balancing that with raising four children, being a class parent, and deciding to build a Girl Scout Troop and lead it.

One of them is so talented she excels at everything she touches. I've never had such nice hair as when she was a hairdresser. Her "Peace Treaties" were my dog's favorite cookies. Now she makes custom wreaths that should be displayed in Better Homes & Gardens. And all this while renovating a house and raising two children.

I mean, come on.

Most days I forget to remind my children to brush their teeth before we, as usual, frantically run out the front door, 10 minutes late, as I toss their backpacks, masks and water bottles at them, pulling my daughter's rat's nest of hair into a scrunchie that I just found under the couch and yelling, "You can't wear the same pants 3 days in a ROW!!!" at my son.

You see my trepidation here, yes?

Stay-at-home-moms? Amazing. Working moms? Amazing.

Me? Not so much.

I feel like I'm in limbo somewhere. I left the career for a dead-end job with an hour-long commute. I don't do anything particularly fulfilling, but I'm also not home enough because I'm always sitting in traffic.

I feel like Amy Adams in the beginning of the movie where she starts making every recipe in Julia Childs' cookbook.

I want to start cooking. I want my kids to look back and say, "Wow, Mom found that cookbook and she cooked her little heart out."

I just have no idea where to start. And writing a book? That's like skipping straight to the coq a vin or the boeuf bourguignon (I just looked both of those up, they seem intricate- and hard to spell).

So that, Mom, is why I can't just "write a book."

It's impossible.

It's insane.

Anyway, see you in Chapter 2.

Owl Poop

Stay with me.

Because 2020 continues to crap all over everyone's best laid plans, we had to cancel our trip to Long Island to see my sweet, chubby, giggly godson for his first birthday. This hit me particularly hard because this is my bonus family.

Never heard of a bonus family? Oh, it's an incredible thing. Five stars. Highly recommend.

These are technically my husband's cousins but we're all in agreement that, in the event of a divorce, I retain my Taco Tuesday dates with Marion in Jersey and get yearly visitation with Ken in Vegas. I get full custody of Jacqi in Long Island. We've carefully crafted our relationship on a foundation of sarcasm, obscure memes, pictures of our kids driving us crazy, and at least one daily anxiety support session while hiding in our kitchens.

You don't just throw that away.

Anyway, for as upset as I was, my kids were none too pleased either, and in my guilty state, I somehow agreed to take them not to the zoo 20 minutes from my house in Western Jersey, but to the one three hours away that borders Delaware.

It went down like this. "Guys, we're not going to Jacqi and Alex's house for Dominic's birthday, I'm so sorry. They have stuffy noses and sore throats. It's probably allergies, but Grandpa just had surgery. Grandma and Grandpa need my help, and if I bring a cold to their house, it could be really bad. We'll visit them another day omg please don't cry ok we'll go wherever you want today! Where would you like to go??"

I'm clearly running a tight ship over here.

Anyway, instead of being at Jacqi & Alex's, cuddling Dominic and playing dress-up with Chloe, I was watching a screech owl slowly turn tail and crap at me.

And that, when we did our usual, "What was your favorite part of today's adventure?" chat, was my 8-year-old's immediate answer.

"When the owl pooped at us- that was so awesome.

On Monday at school when we talk about our week-ends, I'm SO going to tell everyone that we drove to a zoo and an owl turned around and pooped right at us!"

My daughter's favorite part?

"The pepperoni pizza!"

And that, in a nutshell, is why I have no time to write a book.

I'm having too much fun with these weirdos.

I'm having too much fun watching them run through a zoo discussing whether they'd prefer a tamarin or a bison as a pet.

I'm having too much fun playing trivia games with them as we freeze our asses off while waiting for our dinner entrees, because none of us is quite comfy enough to try indoor dining.

Afraid of indoor dining- there's a line I never thought I'd say.

Life is always hectic, but 2020 has been especially WTF-tastic. To keep it a little less "holy shit what is next?!" for the kids, we've been taking them on "adventures" every weekend. We hike, we explore, we shop, we eat, and we laugh. A lot. I honestly don't know many adults that I'd rather spend my time with than my grumpily adorable husband and my owl poo and pepperoni pizza-loving offspring.

Sappy Moment Alert- they complete me.

No, really.

I live for weekends. We plan a trip on Friday night, get up way too early on Saturday, pack a week's worth of snacks (which we will devour before lunch) and go. We hike to castles and drive hours out of our way to find the best vegan cheesecake or gluten free sandwiches (please see Chapter 1 RE: All the Allergies). Pat (the grumpily adorable husband) and I split tastings at obscure breweries while the kids play Minecraft and Pac Man, while munching on Pop Chips and sipping Honest juice boxes like the tiny hipsters they are. We tell fart jokes in the car; gag and frantically roll down windows when one of the kids actually farts; find fun outdoor restaurants for dinner; explore antique shops; and share chocolate truffles from Mom & Pop corner stores.

We even mini-golfed, although that will probably be a one-and-done type situation (I don't want to discuss it).

These are my people. I wouldn't trade them for anything in the world. Nothing.

Not even achieving my goal of becoming a- dramatic sigh- published writer.

Because if I was doing the freelance thing full time, I'd be chained to my laptop all weekend, researching random blog topics to get my 500-word submissions flowing and make my whopping $18/piece. I'd miss all of it- pepperoni pizza with plant-based mozzarella (which is surprisingly believable, by the way); and taking turns picking car songs to obnoxiously belt out on the way to those castles. I'd miss watching them both collapse into fits of giggles upon seeing a bottle of hot sauce in a tiny gift shop in Cape May, NJ, that has butt cheeks on it and reads, "Kiss Your Ass Goodbye." They were so beside themselves that day that I almost had to abandon my "buy 3 for $25" gourmet coffee purchase to get them away from the butt-cheek bottle.

And I don't want to miss a second of it. Not even the owl poop. Because one day, they'll be "over" our weekend adventures. Their friends will take precedence over their boring old parents. "Can we go to a museum?" will be replaced by, "Can I borrow the car?"

And from what I understand, all of that will be swift, abrupt, and pretty damn painful.

So for as long as I have their attention, I will gladly

put off everything else for dilapidated castles with questionable porta-potties, butt cheek hot sauce, and 92 different museums about rocks, dolls, and maritime life in the 1800's.

I'll gladly live my other dream- the "mom who sings off-key to Whitesnake while her kids look on from the back seat in horror" dream.

That will be a dream worth writing about- one day.

CHAPTER 3

The Short Straw

The brightest little ray of sunshine in our house since March- or as I like to refer to it, the moment we transitioned from BC (before Covid) to DC (during Covid)- has been my unshakeable 5-year-old daughter.

Grace has been the rock that we've come to depend on, for her consistency, humor, and easy-going approach towards pandemic living.

The strength and resiliency that this child has shown since March continues to blow my mind.

Preschool let out one day and never resumed?

Mom has to spend all of her time simultaneously teaching 2nd grade and working from the dining room table?

Dad has Covid? On Easter?

No problem!

Every morning, this warrior of a toddler woke up, dressed herself, brushed her teeth, and got her own breakfast. She sat at the dining room table and worked on the preschool workbooks I had hastily ordered on Amazon at the start of the shutdown, while I tried to Google "how many vertices does a parallelogram have?" to prove to my son that he was wrong (he was right, incidentally. Math isn't my thing). She taught herself how to color and write flawlessly. When she tired of her work, she would put the breakfast dishes in the sink, get a snack, and select a movie for herself. She entertained our 65-lb bull-in-a-china-shop dog so that I had fewer messes to clean.

She put herself down for naps.

That's right. NAPS.

When my husband contracted Covid just before Easter, Grace was solid as a cement block. She moved all of her belongings into her brother's room so that her bedroom was ready to be used as my sick room if/when I caught the virus. She spent her days making "get well" crafts for her dad and baking "I LOVE YOU" cutout cookies with frilly pink sprin- kles, for me to leave at the door to our bedroom, where he was isolating. She helped me devil eggs for Easter dinner right after watching him collapse in the backyard (the moment we realized hey, he might be suffering from more than "allergies.")

When she found out we couldn't go anywhere without masks, she donned the first one I gave her, said, "I love this blue one, it reminds me of Frozen!", never complained, and never looked back.

When she found out kindergarten would be mostly virtual, she embraced it all. She bounces into the car on in-person days. She bounces to the computer on virtual days. She attends music class in the dining room, singing and dancing like she's at the best party of her little life. She talks excitedly about things like mask breaks and social distancing story time. She rolls out my yoga mat every Thursday at noon and does 20 minutes of themed yoga for virtual gym class.

This girl is my hero.

Life since March 12th, when my job instructed us "not to return until further notice," has been a hazy nightmare of epic proportions, but that girl has kept this mama focused, determined and centered.

I look at her easy smile and hear her joyous giggles early each morning, and they give me a reason to get out of bed and face another day.

I have come to depend on her innocent strength to lift me from the depression that I've been battling almost every single day of this mess.

Which is why, although I should have been expecting it, I was totally taken aback last week when she threw herself on the ground, face first, when I asked her if I could wash her baby blanket.

It was bound to happen. This kid drew the shortest of short straws, and she's been quietly carrying her burden with more decorum than I could ever muster.

My husband never stopped working (minus the two weeks he was in bed, struggling to breathe). I began working from home and had regular access to my coworkers and friends, virtually, whenever I needed them. I met friends for dinner, chatted with my neighbors as we walked our dogs 18 times a day, and used grocery shopping as "me time." Although to be fair, I've always done that. Trader Joe's, you complete me.

When schools shuttered their doors, my son was able to see his friends through virtual classroom "meetings" each day. I signed him up for Kids Messenger and (very, very grudgingly) downloaded Fortnite so he could still attend "playdates." His in-person karate classes turned into daily one-on-one Zoom sessions. He saw friends at distanced bbqs and the local lake during the summer. When school reopened, he returned to his familiar place, to see all of his familiar faces (well, half of their faces).

My daughter's school, being near my job, is an hour from our house. She had no friends nearby. Her school couldn't do regular meets or lessons (imagine asking twenty 3- and 4-year-olds to sit still in front of a laptop every day). Her preschool graduation was held in my driveway; I handed her a diploma that I created with construction paper and crayons. My neighbors and my parents clapped and handed her flowers. My husband brought home a fancy chocolate cake.

She told me it was the most wonderful graduation she could have ever imagined.

When school reopened, she stepped out of my car to a completely new building, with completely new people, and a completely new routine. She did so with a bounce in her step that is akin to the first time she set foot in Disneyland.

She never got to say goodbye to her amazing teachers or friends. She left school on a Wednesday- and never saw them again.

That is a very real, very traumatic thing.

But this kid- this amazingly tough, resilient kid- never wavered. She marched on.

Which is why it should have been no surprise to me when she marched right into a wall, slid down that wall and landed in a puddle on the floor...over a baby blanket.

"Gracie, can I have Boppy?"

"Why? No."

"I need to wash it."

"I like it this way. It smells like cookies. It's fine."

"Gracie girl, it's been a week, it smells like a hamster, and I need to toss it in the wash."

Cue the dark clouds rolling in over the hazel eyes.

Massive explosion of arms and legs.

Dramatic crash to the ground.

Crack of forehead against dog-claw-scuffed wood floor.

Hysterical, eardrum-splitting sobs.

I'm actually embarrassed by the amount of time I spent standing across the room, frozen in total confusion, before it clicked.

Boppy was her last constant. Her last safe space.

Covid has taken all of her stability away- just pulled the rug right out from under her Size 10 Toddler fuzzy boots.

And she withstood the storm.

She withstood the abrupt separation from the only friends she's ever known.

From the teachers that were like older sisters and extra moms.

From the space she could call her own each day.

She was strong for herself, for us, for so long.

But Boppy is her last safety net. And losing him for even an hour, was losing too much.

I finally understood.

I got down on the floor and scooped her up. I held her shaking body against mine as she wailed, "I miss my old life! I miss my friends, and Miss Kerry, and Miss Brianna, and Miss Melissa! I miss my table and my art stuff! I want my old life back! I never got to say goodbye, Mommy! I just wanted to say goodbye!"

I've held her many nights while she sobbed to me about the loss of her old life- she's strong, but she's not a robot. But I had yet to see a meltdown of this proportion.

And in a way, I was relieved.

Relieved that she was finally letting it all out, and giving into the type of all-encompassing sorrow that we've all had to let into our lives a few times to really process what's happening around us.

We've all thrown ourselves on the ground and pounded our fists at least once to protest the taking away of all of our Boppies.

She was finally protesting the loss of hers.

In the end, I waited two more days to wash that awful, stained, hamster-smelling, shredded old baby blanket. But it gave her the peace of knowing that she can still dictate what happens to at least one of her safety nets.

And after everything she's done for us over the past 8 months, we owe her at least that.

CHAPTER 4

The Follow-Through

I'm really, really great at starting things. I am what you might call a professional at manifesting fantastic ideas. If that was an actual thing that could earn me a living, I'd be a millionaire.

And once I manifest these ideas, I plan the crap outta them.

When I saw an email about a State Employee discount on Universal Studios tickets last year, I not only bought those tickets (before I remembered to tell my husband that we were taking a vacation to Universal Studios)- I turned it into the experience of a lifetime. I typed acceptance letters from Hogwarts and stamped them with the school's official seal. I bought each kid a stuffed owl, which I propped up next to their bedroom doors, holding the letters. I bought treat bags, candies, and fancy tags, and created individual collections of chocolate frogs, Bertie Bott's Every Flavor Beans, gummy slugs, and dragon eggs. I bought chocolate coins in 3 colors and gave them each little change purses of sickles, knuts and galleons. I bought matching Harry Potter pajamas and t-shirts.

I even squeezed a day at Disney World into the middle of our Wizarding World Of Harry Potter week.

Bippity Boppity Boom.

In April, when our Spring Break vacation turned into us quarantining on the first floor while Pat isolated upstairs with the Rona, I decided to put together theme days. We celebrated Thanksgiving, Halloween, Christmas, and Valentine's Day. Each day had movies, games, music, baking, and themed crafts. I'm talking decorated pine cones from our backyard; ghost, gingerbread man, turkey and heart sugar cookies; and a Halloween dance-off on the lawn in front of the neighbors.

On Friday I held the Quarantine Olympics, with 12 events and an obstacle course that I threw together with patio chair cushions, pool noodles, and whatever else I could find in the backyard. We even had a Closing Ceremony on the front porch with leftover 4th of July sparklers.

On Saturday I stress-ate under a blanket on the couch.

Hey. It's impossible to top Quarantine Olympics so why even try?

However, during month 5 of "Oh My God We Still Can't Do Anything," I had a whirlwind week of creativity. I snuck off to Michael's, bought a bag of summer-themed foam stickers, a hole punch, and gold ribbon, and created 200 "decorations." On July 24th I dragged our Christmas tree up from the basement and declared that we were celebrating Christmas in July. I danced and sang along to the Nightmare Before Christmas soundtrack (it IS a Christmas movie and I will debate anyone who disagrees) while the kids giddily hung foam hot dogs, ice cream cones, and burgers, strung shell garlands, and made a star out of rainbow striped pinwheels. The next day I placed a mountain of gifts (wrapped school supplies and clearance summer clothes for the win) under our hot dog tree, and made a feast that would put Martha Stewart to shame- ok, maybe not that great. But I did make a vegan snowman cheeseball with a cute little red pepper scarf.

I was made for complicated, creative, detailed ideas.

I think it's a byproduct of my ever-present, raging anxiety, but that's for my therapist to sort out. You're just here for entertainment, so we'll carry on.

Anyway, jittery creative genius, yes- except when the ideas pertain to...you guessed it...me.

I've started and stopped at least 4 books (maybe 5 if this one goes by the wayside!).

I've started and stopped at least as many different career pursuits (holistic nutritionist had some real steam for awhile. Vegan dessert caterer was the fastest to crash and burn).

I've abandoned countless exercise routines (to be fair, I couldn't continue Tae-Bo in good conscience after almost taking out my aunt's window...and my aunt).

I'm wonky at best when it comes to keeping up with my two blogs.

I'm just not great at the follow-through.

I'm very "pie in the sky" about my career goals- but then I see a piece of pie and abandon my dreams for a snack with a scoop of vanilla and some coconut milk whipped cream.

You know how it is- everyone else...and snacks... take precedence. But when it comes to yourself, eh...it can wait. It'll happen another day.

The kids need education, attention, and enrichment.

The husband needs affection, reassurance, and someone to watch cooking shows with him.

The dog needs walks, pets, meals, and quality time to chase the chipmunks that have set up an entire civilization on my property.

My job needs me to give 110% during business hours, and to lie awake worrying about random work-related things overnight.

My bathroom needs scrubbing and my dishwasher needs a good shaking to keep it from shutting off mid-cycle again.

The recycling needs flattening because apparently my husband, the engineer, is incapable of pressing a milk carton into a flat shape.

The kids' rooms need scouring because apparently, they really do try to dispose of socks in the hamper, but they keep ending up on the floor, in their desks, under their beds, in front of their dressers and, at least once a day, in the dog's mouth (which, if not pulled out, ends up on my lawn 48-72 hours later).

Which reminds me, the yard needs cleaning...

The parents need me to come over at all hours when one of them insists he can liberate himself from his wheelchair to change all 4 lightbulbs in the chandelier over the dining room table (I got 2 electrical shocks and only 1 thank you that night, if anyone's counting…)

So anything that really sparks my interest, fires up my soul, or otherwise gets me excited- it just becomes repeatedly entertained and then abandoned.

Later.

Tomorrow.

After we get through the weekend.

After we get through next week.

After we get through the holidays.

After we get through the pandemic.

After we get through ::insert anything::

Like I said, if it has anything to do with me, I suck at the follow-through.

Like with this writing a book thing that my mom so crazily suggested.

I can tell you right now that it's not going to happen.

I may not even finish this chapter.

As a matter of fact,

CHAPTER 5

Wanted

Anyone else's kids pop up like prairie dogs every time they hear the jingle of keys?

I could fall down the stairs, roll across the living room floor and knock them both over like bowling pins, and as long as they're on their tablets they wouldn't even notice. But the second the house key clinks against the car key?

Pop. "Where are you going?"

Pop. "Why are your shoes on?"

"How long will you be gone?"

"Can we come?"

"Do you have to go?"

Meanwhile, the dog is a giant black and white blur, careening across the room, slamming into the entryway table and scattering LED tealights in every direction, thinking she's going for a walk. Not that I have ever once brought my car keys on a walk around the block- but Marty....she needs her own chapter. Maybe Chapter 6, if I'm still writing by then.

My son is the more prevalent prairie dog for errand-running; his overly-wordy slogan is, "I'll be good, I won't ask for anything, I never get time with just you and me, and if I don't come you won't have anyone to sing with when our favorite songs come on the radio."

Kid drives a hard bargain- I do love a good car singing partner.

My daughter is in charge of showers.

If the linen closet creaks, or the pantry door groans…

Pop.

There she is, like one of the twins in The Shining, smiling at me as I freeze with my towel in one hand and my lemongrass soap in the other.

"Are you taking a shower?"

No, I've decided that this is a better way to shine the furniture.

"Yep."

"Ok let's chat!"

"I'm all good, Gracie, I'm just going to be quick."

"No way, we're girlfriends! Girlfriends chat in the shower!"

I have never taken any of my friendships to that level. Nor have I ever showered with one of my friends, no matter how much she insisted it's "what girlfriends do!" the few times she actually climbed INTO the shower, sat in the back and patted the tub as an invitation to wax poetic while shampoo dripped into my eyes.

But I did. I sat there and talked about my day and listened to her rendition of As the Preschool Turns, the few times she ventured into that 80 year-old bathtub, grinning like she finally understood how to adult.

And every night, when she follows me into the bathroom and sits on the bowl, telling me stories that sometimes last longer than the hot water, I let her.

And when she quietly slides my toothbrush through the shower curtain onto the back ledge of the tub, lovingly pre-loaded with what my kids refer to as "Mom's weird, smelly toothpaste" (it's fennel, guys. It's not that exotic), my heart bursts a little bit.

And my son? His campaign slogan almost always gets him elected to the Backseat Singing Committee.

Because honestly, they're right. I don't get a ton of time alone with Vince, and, since at the ripe old age of 8 years, he already rejects hand-holding and public hugging, I'm not sure how much more time I have before he refuses to go anywhere with me.

And my daughter really is my best little girlfriend. I love her run-on stories, her original songs, and her genuine interest in all things Mommy, right down to how much weird fennel toothpaste I prefer on my toothbrush.

I like being wanted.

After all, I grew these people. I knew them before anyone else ever laid eyes on them. Why wouldn't I want to soak in every second I can before we go from, "Mommy, want to chat?" to "Ma, leave me alone!" (I will cry on that day. I will ground them for using that tone...but then I will cry)

My husband does his best to make sure I get time to regroup- especially this year. It's been just the three of us (and Marty the LED tealight destroyer), all day, every day, since March. Wake up together; do schoolwork together; eat every meal together; take the dog for walks together; fold laundry together...

soothe each other's tantrums with each other. And there are plenty of them.

Mine are probably the worst.

By the time Pat strolls through the door each night I'm what I believe other moms refer to as "touched out." I'm pretty sure that even though I'm smiling and asking about his day, all he sees is a woman that slightly resembles the 22-year-old girl he married, but also looks eerily similar to a rabid racoon in one-size-too-big pajama pants.

So naturally the guy thinks my sanity depends on getting away from those kids for a while.

So, also naturally, his own sanity is challenged when I get annoyed as he chases said children out of the bathroom or firmly declares, "You are not going to Target with your mother!"

It's such a weird dichotomy, isn't it, this parenthood thing? You spend so much time fantasizing about all that alone time you used to have, but you don't really want it so much anymore.

And to be honest, I'm not sure I like whatever scenario would come to be if I did take too much time to myself. Grace still can't rinse the shampoo out of her hair; Vince has a knack for getting put into timeout if I'm gone for even 8 minutes; the dog panics if I go outside without her and categorically refuses to poop for my husband; and my husband... for a fiercely independent, quiet to the point of being mime-like, man, he is also, secretly, the cuddliest one of them all.

I wrote the first four chapters of this book from 12-3am on a Sunday morning because that is the only time of day or night when I was guaranteed that no one could possibly need me...or so I thought.

I was in the zone, typing away with such zest that the keyboard was practically smoking, breaking only to dip another "I can eat as many chicken nuggets as I want because it's 2:30 in the morning" chicken nugget in barbecue sauce. This was it. I was alone! I was doing my thing! I might write this entire book by morning!

Creak.

I froze. It wasn't a kid...it was coming from upstairs.

But why? It was 2:30 in the morning! My guaranteed time!

"Hey, it's 2:30 in the morning...everything ok?"

It was my blearly-eyed, secretly cuddly husband.

"Everything is fine...I was trying to write."

"Oh...ok."

"Are you ok?"

"I'm fine...just having trouble sleeping."

He could go the rest of his life not setting foot in a Target, he's not one for chatting in the shower...or really, ever...and, thank God because this would be a deal-breaker- he has never asked me to hang out with him while he poops.

But I guess that bed is pretty big without his little spoon.

I bit back a smile, finished up my obscene pile of Trader Joe's nuggets, licked the bbq sauce off the plate (2:30 in the morning rule, don't you judge me), and washed up for bed. There'd be "me" time tomorrow- maybe at midnight, but I'd take it.

Because at the end of the day (or ridiculously early the next morning), it feels pretty great to be wanted.

CHAPTER 6

Marty Maraschino

Let's talk about the dog.

This dog is not what I wanted.

I campaigned against adopting this dog.

This dog is as unwieldy as a dozen eggs rolling around on the hood of a moving car, and as destructive as that moving car driving through an antique store.

She eats anything- and I mean anything- she can get her paws on. Crayons are her favorite appetizer. Toilet paper straight off the roll is the joy of her life. But socks, those are her caviar.

I've caught her gnawing on my wood floors more than once, lips curled back, face planted to the ground, staring at me with a strange kind of guilty, toothy, skeletal grin.

She peed on the basement floor yesterday, presumably because I was taking too long switching the laundry when I should have been taking her for a walk in the rain.

She growls as a sign of affection and cries when she's happy. We think she was wired backwards.

She gets so excited when we wake up in the morning that she slams her body on top of ours and repeatedly smacks our faces with her freakishly-long limbs and bony paws.

Her hashtag on my social media posts is #martythemenace.

I did not. Want. This dog.

And I absolutely cannot live without her.

Marty came into our lives very unexpectedly, and if it had been up to me, she wouldn't have come in at all. I can't even remember how many times I repeated, "We don't need another dog. We can't have another dog. We already have a dog."

And as I determinedly but futilely repeated myself, my husband and 2 kids were on the floor- my 6ft, 200lb husband was ON THE FLOOR- of the Petco, cooing over this little, wiggly, mushy puppy.

And- here's the kicker- the puppy wasn't even her!

I pulled every one of them off the floor, politely explained to the rescue group that we already had a dog, a senior dog who, by the way, hated other dogs, and that we both worked an hour from home and didn't have a fenced-in yard, so we were awful candidates. I wished them well and shared my sincere hopes that Sandy the black lab/bluetick hound puppy would find her forever home.

Three days later, Marty Maraschino waltzed into my house. And promptly peed on the floor.

I never stood a chance.

My family- they're crafty little buggers. They started before I had even clicked my seatbelt.

"A puppy is perfect! She could be Rocco's friend!"

"She was so soft and snuggly, Mommy!"

"We would be saving her!"

My husband was quiet- he waited to deliver the final blow. He paced himself. He let the kids move all the pawns out of the way during the drive home. Then he set up the laptop in the dining room, handed me a glass of wine, and gently said, "Rocco is getting older, Cath. A puppy might keep him young for a little longer. And…when his time comes…the house won't be so empty. It might make it easier on the kids…and us."

That. Bastard.

Checkmate.

So I drank that wine and I filled out that application. But I had a few moves up my sleeve- I was brutally honest. I detailed Rocco's medical issues, his hatred of other dogs, our lack of a fence, alllll the hours we were out of the house each day. They thought they could manipulate me. HA! I knew I'd never hear from that rescue again.

Long story short, Marty moved in 3 days later, we formally adopted her just before Christmas 2017, and I've been a freelance writer for the rescue ever since.

And I've never been so happy about being so wrong.

That unhinged, untrainable animal riled up our old dachshund so much that he started to exhibit energy I hadn't seen since he was a puppy. I watched him, all 11 pounds of him, chase that floopy, dopey puppy around the dining room table until they both collapsed. I watched him steal her toys, and could swear I heard him laughing evilly as he trotted away with them. I watched him- I hope he can forgive me for sharing this- cuddle with her.

And on that Sunday night just 3 weeks before his 14th birthday, when Rocco told us it was time for him to leave, I watched Marty Maraschino become a completely different dog.

We had loved her from the second she wobbled through our door- we spoiled her with toys, took her on long walks, and gave her endless amounts of cuddles- but I think Marty always knew she was the "second" dog. We had adopted Rocco when he was only 5 months old- he was our first baby. We were barely 22 years old, he was barely the size of our forearms, and the three of us became a family together.

He protected my belly through 2 pregnancies; I held, hand fed, and massaged his little limbs and back through a myriad of chronic health issues. We had birthday parties for this dog- and our friends and family showed up with gifts. When he passed, no one could dry our tears because they were sobbing right along with us.

This dog was one in a million. No one would ever replace him.

So Marty never tried.

Instead, she loved him right along with us- and she paid attention. And when the time came, she quietly, gently stepped in.

Two days after Rocco died, as Vince and I were settling into his bed for our nightly Harry Potter chapter, I heard the quietest footsteps approaching his door. Ditching her usual pony-like romp, Marty gently stepped onto his bed, curled up next to him, and put her head on his lap. Rocco's nightly spot. She's been there every night since.

The first time Gracie sat on the living room floor to watch a movie and realized she would be without her lap-sized cinema partner (and snack stealer), Marty got up from her favorite corner, plopped down next to Grace, and let her rhythmically pet the same patch of fur for almost two hours (and she didn't steal a single snack, although I did see Grace's free hand sliding from the popcorn bowl to the dog's mouth every few minutes...).

She let me bury my head in her chest to sob time and time again and, as a nice change, didn't accidentally knock me in the head with her jaw.

She was basically the Aaron Rodgers to Rocco's Brett Favre.

So she threw up a sock- onto Vince's bed- while Vince was in it...at 4 o'clock this morning.

So she's currently snoring, drooling and farting on my couch as I type this.

So my house is scuffed, chewed up, and constantly smells like zoo animal.

So she trampled me in bed yesterday morning and, I'm fairly certain, bruised my spleen with her butt bone.

She's my dog. The one I didn't want. The one I resisted.

The one who stole my heart, and healed it.

CHAPTER 7

This Old House

When I was a kid, one of my favorite movies was *The Money Pit*, a disastrous comedy about a young couple who buys a home together and then struggles to keep it from falling apart. I remember watching it with my mom, the two of us laughing so hard that tears stained our 1980's sweatshirts, our hands slapping the knees of our scrunchie-sock covered stirrup leggings.

It was so funny because it just seemed so far-fetched, especially to a naïve 6-year-old who knew nothing of home improvement beyond the fact that my dad could (and did) fix anything that threatened to crumble in whichever house we were renting.

Because of course, that would NEVER be my situation. Noooo, when I was an adult, I would be a famous literary darling, have a robust savings account, and buy a beautiful little house in the country that smelled like cinnamon and had a warm, welcoming dining room where everyone gathered.

And of course, I would own that house, with my husband and our 2 children, by the time I was 30. It would have a nice yard with a white wooden picket fence for our 2 dogs. And I would sit on the porch with a notebook, a freshly-sharpened pencil, and a piping hot mug of herbal tea, writing my novels in twirly script.

I thought about that movie as I walked into the living room last Sunday to see the muffin-sized hole near my living room ceiling, where my husband had finally given up on ever getting the 70-year-old curtain hardware out, and had just grabbed it and pulled.

I thought about it again 20 minutes later as I watched a sheet of tiles, clearly terrified that they were about to be re-caulked, careen off the wall in an elegant swansong and land in my bathtub.

I thought about it this morning when I walked into the dining room and found that an apparition- because both children vehemently denied involvement- had put something that looked suspiciously the same size as a chair leg through the plaster wall.

Turns out, *The Money Pit* wasn't so far-fetched.

Because, while the tub hasn't come crashing through the basement ceiling (yet), on some level I'm Shelley Long and my husband, Pat, is Tom Hanks.

We have our very own money pit.

My dream of owning a charming old country house came true- I just wasn't prepared for the level of "old" I'd be dealing with.

The plaster walls are like the Mona Lisa- they appear smooth, freshly painted and full of cheeky family photos, but the closer you get, the more they look like cracked hard-boiled eggs.

Sitting too near a window in the winter months will give you a breeze so strong that your hair will look like Marilyn Monroe's dress when she stepped on that grate.

My white wooden picket fence is a rotted brown and green algae color. It's missing a few pieces where a bear decided it was in his way a few weeks ago.

Apparently, I have disciplined myself enough to write the book, but my porch is uncovered and full of flies, my handwriting is illegible, and I have those 2 children, a full-time job, and a pandemic to deal with. Soooo I'm doing it in the middle of the night on a laptop, bleary-eyed and typing to the rhythm of the ancient water pressure tank clicking on and off every 5 minutes. And eating chicken nuggets, of course.

And it's a thousand times more fulfilling that anything I imagined at the ripe old age of six.

Sure, living in a house that was built almost 100 years ago and never properly updated has its own level of stress. Will the kitchen light turn on today? Will that crack in the garage wall survive another storm? If I close that window, will it ever open again? Why does that basement light smell when it's on for more than 10 minutes? And one of my personal favorites- why is the floor squishy over there?

But then there's this other side of it- the fun, challenging, exhilarating thrill of fixing things.

Pat and I refer to it as This Old House, and we take turns playing Bob Villa whenever something threatens to declare mutiny.

The look of pride on his face when he brushed the last bit of stain on the patio that he designed and created, was so fun to see. The first time we roasted marshmallows and clinked our whiskey glasses around the fire pit that we built together-that was pretty cool.

The exhilaration we got from resizing a hole in the wall to fit the new AC we purchased 2 summers ago is almost embarrassing. I danced over the peel & stick tiles I stuck over the old linoleum in the kitchen because I loved them so much. $40, 20 minutes and so much joy. What can I say? I like cheap thrills.

Which brings me to the tiles.

I can spackle like a ninja and lay an entire floor while dinner cooks. I can paint window molding with my eyes closed and reorganize rooms-full of furniture to hide cracks in 1950's-era plaster walls.

But bathrooms terrify me.

I remember watching my father re-tile our bathrooms over, and over, and over again, all to no avail. I remember taking showers with plastic tarps and tape rubbing against my legs while the latest round of re-grouting dried. I imagine a geyser of water erupting out of the floor if we try to replace the massive, "sometimes I flush, sometimes I don't" toilet. I have nightmares about removing the vanity to find a color of mold science has yet to discover.

So, as much as Pat has wanted to tackle it, that is one room I refused to touch. My goal has been to spit, tape and glue it all together until we can afford that magical word- Contractor.

But those four tiles were onto me, and they blew my plan right out of the water.

My first reaction, of course, was to do the adult thing and fly into a panic.

"If I touch that wall the tiles are all going to fall down, like an old, moldy, ceramic waterfall! We can't fix this. I'm taking out a $10,000 loan. We're gutting it. I've reached my limit."

But Pat knew I could do this, and that I needed to. I needed to face my childhood tape and tarp trauma. I needed to fix those tiles.

This was my shining Bob Villa moment.

So, like the hopeless romantic that he is, he kissed me, handed me the electric drill, and dashed off in the mommy-mobile into the homeowner's Dark Forest that is Home Depot. He returned with a little bucket of cement, a fun-looking spatula thingy and a tube of grout, put them on the sink and smiled that smirky smile of his. Then he uttered the words that make every girl weak in the knees- "Make sure you cover the entire tile before you stick it to the wall."

Scared though I was, I Bob Villa'ed the hell out of those stupid tiles. I attached my little grout-cleaning brush to the drill and drilled my heart out until the grout around that gaping hole in my wall was as white as a new tooth. I caulked cracks. I sealed things. I mixed cement and slathered it all over those tiles-which promptly fell back off the wall a few times but nonetheless, I kept at it. At last, I proudly popped the last tile into place…and watched the other three pop back off the wall.

But in the end, I won the battle. Covered in caulk, cement, and tile cleaner, I stood back and admired my work.

They aren't completely flush with the wall. The grout and caulk look like they were applied by an overtired 3-year-old. And the one on the end looks a bit like a loose tooth that's one apple away from abandoning ship.

But I did it. I fixed my old house, all by myself. I proudly taped and tarped the wall, and then took a shower with it clinging to my leg…. ahh, just like old times.

Every day for the past week, every time I walk into the bathroom, I look at that half-assed repair job and I grin from ear to ear. It's not pretty. It's probably not very sturdy.

But it's mine.

The walls are old plaster; the electrical is questionable; and our bed may one day crash into the living room. But it's warm, it smells like whatever candle burns brightly each night, and it has a nice big dining room table that just loves to be surrounded by guests.

This old house…is perfect just the way it is.

CHAPTER 8

Ernie McJingles

"**I** can't wait to start my list for Santa!"

"Mommy is Santa!"

Ahhh, the joys of having an older sibling.

Let me set the scene for you. We're strolling through the streets of Lake George, browsing the shops while we wait for our gas station chicken gyros to be ready (I'll explain later). I'm asking the kids what they might want for Christmas in a few months, telling them to start getting their lists ready for St. Nick. I'm reveling in the joy that is window shopping on a crisp autumn day, watching my little ones' eyes light up at the mention of the upcoming holidays. I'm smug as….well, something that's really smug…at the way I whipped up a low budget, social distance-friendly weekend getaway during both leaf peeping season and a pandemic, to give them some joy and fresh air amidst the chaos of 2020.

I'm happy as a clam, thinking about planning a quiet Christmas at home, baking a feast with all the trimmings, and wrapping up those special gifts from Santa & Mrs. Claus in special paper, with special handwriting...I'm feeling all sorts of cozy. And in the middle of my reverie, Vince drops the truth bomb. Not once, but twice.

And he dropped it in song.

"Mommy is SaAantaAa!"

I stopped so abruptly that if we had been closer to the lake, whoever was behind me would have bounced off my ass and fallen in.

"Um, what? Vince, are you serious? Where would you even get an idea like that? How could I fly all over the world in one night, dude?"

"Oh, I'm just kidding, Mommy!"

But he wasn't, and I knew it.

I can sense bullshit when it emanates from one of my darling little children, and that kid REEKED of lies.

I let it go. I bought Gracie some new bows for her hair and searched through a box of Fortnite keychains for Vince's favorite, Beef Boss (I have no idea who or what s/he is, but the fact that we both squealed in the middle of the comic book shop when I found it tells you I'm way too invested in that stupid game). I let it go while we hungrily chowed down on our gas station chicken gyro platters (again, later). I let it go for the rest of our trip. I let it churn around and stew in the back of my mind for days after we returned home to hybrid schooling and daily covid count updates.

I waited for him to come to me. When he didn't, I dropped the hammer at bedtime one night the following week.

"What book do you want to read tonight, Bud?"

"How about the one about Jackie Robinson? I love that one."

"Me too! Do you want a snack?"

"Sure! Want to share some peanut butter crackers while we read?"

"Absolutely! You don't believe in Santa, do you?"

".........what?"

"Vince."

"Ok. No, I don't. I'm sorry."

And then he let it all pour out.

How he stumbled into the completely off-limits, 100% forbidden, "Go in there and I will cancel Christmas" gift-wrapping room last Christmas Eve and saw a shiny pink scooter for Gracie. How that same scooter was propped up against the tree the next morning- in Santa's special paper, with Santa's special handwriting.

"I didn't want to say anything, because I didn't want to make you sad. But I thought about it and thought about it, and the only thing that made sense is that you must be Santa. Like, that Santa is just a story and you really do all this stuff."

He looked at me timidly, almost sadly. I was completely heartbroken. I could see his innocence floating out the bedroom window.

"I mean, obviously I know the Tooth Fairy, the Easter Bunny, and Jack Frost are totally real...but I think you're Santa."

Wait! Shut the window- there was hope!

Just like the Grinch, I was so sly and so slick...and so desperate...I thought up a lie, and I thought it up quick.

"Bud," I began, taking a deep breath, "I need to tell you something."

All the air left his lungs. I watched him deflate like an old birthday balloon.

"I'm ready, Mom."

"Vinny, I bought that scooter. Not Santa."

I could see tears forming. "I knew it."

"Last year was a rough one for him. His elves were working overtime, but there were so many good kids, and so much demand for certain things. That scooter was at the top of a bunch of kids' lists, and he just ran out of time and supplies. He emailed me to let me know he was going to fall short, and asked if there was anything else Gracie was really wishing for. But I knew how badly she wanted it, and I was able to find it in a store so I grabbed it. I told him I'd leave it in the sun room for him to wrap and tag, and he did."

My heart was pounding. I was trying to keep a straight face. There was no way he was going to buy this.

But he looked up at me with a mixture of hope and hesitation, and of course a hint of his new, trademark skepticism (he gets that from his father).

"Wait...Santa can run out of stuff?"

"Vinny, he's magical. He's not God. Of course. It rarely happens, but it does. So I filled in the gaps."

"So...he is real? Really?"

"Bud, I know you're reaching an age where you're going to start questioning things. And I know your friends are going to start telling you that a lot of what you believe isn't real. But I believe. I believe he is real. And I hope that at least for another year or two, you will too."

"I...I want to believe, Mommy."

I wanted him to believe too. Not because I wanted to perpetuate something that isn't true. But because... well, because Santa was the source of so much magic in my house when I was a child. Learning that it was all a story was like shattering a glass bubble. It was a piece of my innocence that I never got back. And I wanted him to hold onto every bit of innocence and magic that he possibly could- especially now, in a world so turbulent and frightening that most days I wish I still possessed that glass bubble myself.

"I'll tell you what," I suggested, looking up at the ceiling. "Santa, we have a possible non-believer here. He's had a rough year- we all have- and I'd really like for you to restore his faith in magic. If you're real, can you please send us something, anything, to prove it?"

"Maybe snow!" He was starting to look hopeful.

"Bud, it's the middle of October. I'm not sure he could pull that off! How about...oh God, I don't know....oh wait I know! I want cookie cutters!"

He giggled. "Cookie cutters?! Mommy Santa can't mail cookie cutters, just out of nowhere!"

I laughed with him. "I mean, maybe he can! I have all those plastic cookie cutters, right? But we always have so much trouble getting them through that gluten free dough. I really, really could use some real, high quality, metal cookie cutters. Come on, Santa! Make it happen, for Vince!"

We both laughed, shrugged our shoulders, and read a few chapters about Jackie Robinson. I gave him a big kiss and hug, told him I loved him, and tiptoed out of his room as he drifted off to sleep...

And then I smirked and danced all through the house.

You see, Dear Reader, I already had those cookie cutters. (mwahahahaha)

My friend Crystal recently started a business; she creates and ships custom holiday crafts. As luck would have it, I had just received her latest- a shiny red box containing a letter from the North Pole, some holiday pencils, a checklist of good deeds to send back to Santa, and a few cookie recipes...with shiny, metal, cookie cutters.

The box was wrapped with twine and fitted with an ornate tag. The sender was one Mr. Ernie McJingles.

Me and old Ernie were about to give Vince a little magic.

I waited 3 days and then made my move. The kids were nestled all snug in Vince's room, getting along for the moment, when I brushed past his door with a stack of empty cardboard food boxes, grumbling about how no one else in the house seemed to know how to take the recycling out. That's when I made my move.

Rushing back into the house, I made a beeline for Vince.

"Vince. Be honest. Did you do this?"

"Do what? What is that?"

"I don't know- I went outside to toss the recycling in the garage and this was sitting on the hay bale by the porch. It says it's from an Ernie...Ernie...I can't read this handwriting. Ernie...McTingles...McSingles..."

"It looks like McJingles...Ernie McJingles...Mommy it says it's from the North Pole!"

"Oh my God OHMYGOD! Vince! We need to open it!"

"Yes! What do you think it is???"

"I have no idea!"

"I'll get the scissors; you get Gracie Girl!"

"Ok, Bud!"

Pat, thoroughly confused, watched from the safe distance of the couch.

Vince carefully cut the twine and the kids opened the shiny red box. They removed the letter and grew red-cheeked and giddy as I read it to them. They pored over the good deeds list, bounced around as they pulled out pencils and stickers, and oohed and ahhed over the cookie recipes.

And then....bingo.

"There's more...they're...cookie cutters. Mommy! Cookie cutters..."

"Oh my God, Vince! Metal cookie cutters! It is...it really is..."

"Mommy he heard us! He sent you cookie cutters! He is real!"

I teared up and hugged him. "Vince this is crazy! He is real! I'm crying right now!"

And I was crying, but not for the reasons he thought.

Vince is 8 years old. Gracie is 5. I have a few years of magic left, if I'm lucky. Their friends will disillusion them. Their common sense will win out over their sense of wonder. The elves that I carefully pose each night into theatrical and humorous antics will no longer amaze and delight them. And those red-cheeked, bright-eyed Christmas mornings of "Santa was HERE!" will be replaced by a slightly more sedate, "Thanks Mom and Dad." But for now- for this moment- they still believed in magic. In a world where magic is so very scarce- they still hold it in their hearts.

And, seeing the pure joy radiating from their little faces, I found a little in my own heart.

Thanks, Ernie McJingles, for delivering to us a lot more than cookie cutters. Thanks for returning my glass bubble, even for just a little while longer. I'll hold onto it carefully, I promise.

CHAPTER 9

Gas Station Gyros

We're in the middle of a Social Studies project. Vince can't find his extra fine point black marker. The extra fine point is the only one suitable for perfectly outlining his country, Castle Island. Not the regular point or the fine point (both of which we located, naturally). Just the extra fine point black marker. That is apparently the "it" marker for all fictitious country/island outlining. The extra fine. The crème de la crème of Sharpies. The one that's currently on the lamb.

He's on the verge of tears. Pat's on the verge of an f-bomb. I'm on the verge of hyperventilating.

Not because of the marker. Well, maybe a little because of the marker. I believe the words, "This is why we tell you to put things back after you use them!" have spewed forth from my mouth about 5 times in as many minutes. But no, it's not so much the super fancy marker with the super sharp point.

It's today. Ugh, today was way too Wednesdayish for my liking.

My sister called me, crying, after an argument with my father.

My bonus mom had to cancel our dinner plans. (Bonus Mom: godmother of the husband; embraces woman he marries when mother-in-law declares war on her. Shares many meals, glasses of wine, advice and hugs. Advocates for mother-in-law until cease fire is declared. See Also- Saint.)*

We're a week away from a presidential election that is sure to plunge the country into mass chaos no matter the outcome.

Covid seems to be having the time of its population-infecting life right now.

My doctor told me I may need to be screened for lymphoma.

My car radio was doing a weird thing on the way home.

Ok, we can count the lymphoma thing twice because...for obvious reasons.**

So I'm currently rummaging through the pretty little woven baskets on the top of the fridge that cleverly conceal all of our junk, searching in vain for this ridiculous marker, and trying to keep my breathing steady.

Blue, pink, purple...what if it is lymphoma? Who knew hot flashes were a symptom of cancer? Let it be super early menopause. Or cholesterol! Green, orange...where the fuck is this black marker?! What if this is my last class project? What if the tests come back shouting, "She has Cancer!" Brown... black! Damnit...regular tip. What if this is my last....

"Vacation." I mouthed the word as my eye caught a small wooden knife nestled at the bottom of the basket of every color marker in the world except black.

That little wooden knife had captivated Vince's attention so completely during our last day in Maine this past August. We had spent eight days driving all over the state- fishing in remote ponds while loons called to us from across the water; swimming in ice cold lakes while the sun shone on our backs; and hiking so many beautiful trails we lost count. By that last day, the day we made our long, slow trek back to Jersey, we were exhausted. And hungry. We had gotten to Portland just before dinnertime- and encountered crowds that I was not prepared for. All of the restaurants I had researched for our "last vacation dinner" were slammed with wait lists. We had driven around aimlessly, starting to worry that our last vacation dinner might be whatever we could find at a highway rest stop, when Pat spotted the barbecue place on a side road.

We plopped our hungry, cranky butts onto a picnic bench and ordered the 1.5lb family platter of meats that we don't even eat, and when it came....let's just say not much was left on that platter when we were done. And Vince was begging me to slip a knife in my purse.

In show of environmental awareness and Covid safety, the restaurant was using disposable wooden utensils, and for some reason, the knife was "the coolest thing ever!" according to my kids. While we were waiting for our food Vince had declared he would be decorating it and hanging it on his wall at home. We told him about how ice cream trucks used to sell little cups of vanilla and chocolate with wooden paddles that were just as magical to a little kid. And the little tables that used to come in the pizza box...that blew his mind.

By the end of our meal, we were sharing stories, posing ideas for the little wooden utensil (sharp bookmark to deter book thieves, anyone?), and laughing so hard we had to wipe our eyes with our delicious barbecue-covered napkins. That unassuming little piece of wood changed our entire night. As I slid it into my purse, we decided we did still have some energy, and off to New Hampshire we went.

We were in Maine for eight days. We did so much that I could probably write a book just about that trip. But one of our favorite memories will always be our fantastic 1.5lb barbecue feast on the way home.

Which brings me to the gas station chicken gyros.

We've never been leaf peeping- actually I don't think I've ever even heard that term until this past summer. I was chatting with the owner of a little sandwich shop in a town in Northern Maine while I waited for my lobster roll, and she mentioned that the end of summer was her quiet time before the leaf peepers arrived in the fall.

"They come up here in droves to see the leaves changing color. It's great to be busy, and I love to meet people. Then I prepare for the snowbirds."

"Ugh, I've never been one for crowds- I just enjoy the leaves from my yard," I laughed in reply.

But as October rolled around and social distancing and virtual school began to wear me down again, those leaves began to taunt me through my dining room window. They were begging to be peeped.

So, as usually happens when I get an idea in my restless mind....I put dinner on the stove, searched the halfway point between my town and Lake George, and started looking up hotels in Albany. By the time the dinner dishes were in the sink I had planned an entire low-budget, family friendly weekend of- you guessed it- leaf peeping.

I had great plans for the weekend. Exploring Tarrytown and Beacon, NY on the way. Browsing the stalls at the Tarrytown/Sleepy Hollow Farmer's Market. Eating lunch at Beacon Falls Café, where Pat and I used to have date nights at the corner table by the window. Showing the kids the art gallery where my artist friend had his gallery opening, featuring paintings of their old mama (once upon a time I was cool). Checking into the hotel and heading to this great-looking grill for a fun dinner and a stroll to the Capitol. Then heading to Lake George the next day for some hiking, strolling along the lake and maybe enjoying a quiet brunch at my Aunt Cathy & Uncle Mike's favorite pancake house, The Silo.

Well, some of my adventures are slam dunks (Jersey to Annapolis to Richmond to Savannah- WITH a surprise visit from the kids' favorite uncle- to Orlando was award-winning, if I do say so myself); and some of them...go the way of leaf peeping.

The farmer's market had nothing allergy-friendly. Beacon Falls Café was packed like a sardine can; and the gallery I couldn't wait to show the kids...it was sold. When we got to the hotel in Albany there was a mix-up with our room, and by the time we got to the fun restaurant that didn't take reservations, they were booked for the night. So the next morning, when we drove the hour to Lake George and found that The Silo had a 60+ minute wait for pancakes, I started to panic.

Pat saw the "here we go again" look of anxiety on my face and put his hand in mine.

"We had a great night last night- that pub had really good food, and the city was nice all lit up. We'll have a great day today. We'll find a place."

The problem was, there were no places that weren't packed to capacity. And THAT is why, as a rule, I am not a leaf peeper. Crowds. Ugh, do not recommend. But given the current situation, I had naively assumed that fewer people would be traveling.

News flash- I was wrong.

After driving up and down the streets of Lake George, unable to even find a parking spot, I finally found a website for a place about a mile away from the mayhem. "The Facebook page has great reviews! It's a gyro and falafel restaurant. Oh, the outdoor balcony looks so nice! Let's try it!"

Starving and hopeful, we plugged the address into the GPS...and arrived, one mile later, at a Sunoco Station.

"No, that can't be right. It's supposed to be- oh, it's right there. It's...in the gas station."

There it was, in all it's 5-star Facebook review glory, attached to the convenience store in the Sunoco Station parking lot.

Spice Gyro and Falafel.

I mean, why not?

This place was so popular that the wait for takeout was 35 minutes. And as soon as I got my plastic bag with gyros wrapped in foil and walked up the stairs to the balcony overlooking the gas pumps, I knew exactly why.

Pat and I are self-proclaimed foodies. We love food. All kinds of food. We love trying it, cooking it, experimenting with it. We've been known to drive 2 hours just to try a pizza place. And, after the massive amounts of food I've woofed down in my 37 years, I can honestly say that these gyros were hands-down the best gyros we have ever eaten.

Gas station chicken gyros.

This food was so good that my kids, who lately have started balking at anything that isn't a Trader Joe's turkey corn dog, were wrapping their chicken kebabs in lettuce, pouring rice over it, and devouring it like they'd never seen food.

Gas. Station. Gyros.

Why am I forcing you to hear about what we eat on vacation?

Because I really need to stress how much we love to eat, yes. But more importantly, because this is the answer to everyone's question.

A question I get a lot.

"How do you plan all these cool trips? How do you find all of these out of the way places?"

Basically, it's a combination of insomnia, Google searches, my fervent desire to avoid crowds, and aimless wandering once we get to whatever destination I cook up at 1am on a random Tuesday.

And regardless of whether the adventure is "flying to Vegas to visit cousin Ken and detouring to Disneyland for 2 days" big, or "leaving at 8am to hike to an obscure waterfall in Connecticut with a bagged lunch" small, it is always, ALWAYS the tiny, unexpected moments that make our trips.

It doesn't matter where you go, or how much you spend. An adventure can be anything, as long as you're together, making memories.

We aren't wealthy; we aren't professional planners; and we aren't a perfect family. We just love to spend time together, doing anything at all.

Laughing over wooden utensils at a bbq place in Portland. Wiping tzatziki sauce off each other's faces at a gas station in Lake George. Pointing out our favorite flowers at a quiet arboretum 28 minutes from our house on a chilly Saturday morning.

It doesn't matter where, or when. Just make the memories.

Maybe I have a million wooden knife and gas station gyro moments left with my little road dogs.

Maybe I've eaten my last lobster roll while chatting about Maine tourism with a sandwich shop owner.

You never know- so don't waste a moment.

Don't wait until you have the money for the "big trips."

Don't wait until you can get reservations at the fancy restaurants.

Make the time and live for the little moments.

Eat the gas station gyros.

Make the memories.

Now if you'll excuse me, I have to find that black marker.

*My mother-in-law is a lovely woman.
**It wasn't lymphoma.

CHAPTER 10

Coffee Run

"**A**re you sure it's her?"

"Yes, it's her, let's go!"

"THANK YOU!"

I was fumbling with my keys and trying not to drop my decaf almond milk 2-pump bourbon caramel pumpkin latte (I always apologize to my barista) on my boots when I heard the chorus of grateful voices from across the street.

My breath caught in my throat as I turned to see the group of them, smiling and waving vigorously across the busy main street, calling, "Thank you so much!!"

Reader, you've been through 9 chapters with me. You know what happened next.

I waved back, yelling, "You are so welcome! Have a

great day!" Then I fumbled my keys and my purse and my boots and my allergy-friendly latte into my Kia and sobbed.

And now for the part of the chapter where I go completely off-topic, possibly throw you off a bit, take the scenic route, and then circle back to my almost always-elusive point.

There's this episode of Friends- Season 5, Episode 4 (in the words of Chandler Bing, could I BE any more obsessed?), that centers around Joey and Phoebe arguing about good deeds. Joey's argument is that there is no such thing as a selfless good deed- because performing them always makes us feel good. So in a way, all good deeds are inherently selfish.

Who knew a 90's sitcom could be so insightful?

Anyway, Phoebe and Joey bet $200 that she can't find a selfless good deed, and she spends the entire episode trying to prove Joey wrong. In the process she gets "force-fed" cider and cookies as a thank you for raking leaves, and eventually even lets a bee sting her- but to no avail. She can't seem to find a completely selfless good deed, and she loses the bet.

My take on this? And why am I talking about a tv sitcom episode from 1998?

Because I think the concept of the "selfless good deed" is very interesting. I don't think there is really such a thing as a selfless good deed. Good deeds inherently make us happy- because we've made someone else happy. Makes sense, right?

My other take on it?

Bring on the selfish good deeds!

Why not spend all damn day making other people happy and giving yourself that warm, fuzzy feeling? Lord knows we could all use some warm and fuzzy right now (hey there, dumpster fire that is 2020…).

Which brings me to my coffee run.

So there I am, sitting in the mommy-mobile, trying to sip my coffee and set my GPS for the office while tears are running down my face like toddlers with an uncapped permanent marker.

A week prior, I had gone on my weekly Tuesday coffee run on my way to work ($5 of self-care to celebrate the kids going back to school/me getting to see my office two days per week), and I had noticed them again. The same group of guys that I saw every Tuesday and Wednesday morning at 8:15am, sitting at tables outside the coffee shop, masked and distanced, laughing, chatting, and sipping coffee.

Every Tuesday and Wednesday, without fail, they were there.

Every time I saw them, I thought about my own friends, who I hadn't seen since February.

The friends I had grown up with, and the friends whose kids my kids were growing up with.

I missed coffee dates and wine nights and playdates-I missed that kinship so much. Seeing these guys making the commitment to spend their mornings together gave me memories of my own lifelong friends. It reminded me that I will get to see them, and hug them, and share a bottle of wine or a pot of coffee with them again.

I was so grateful to them for sitting outside that coffee shop every morning and giving me hope.

So when I went inside to order my usual, I also bought a gift card for $35 to cover the coffee for their next meeting.

As I left the shop, I turned toward their tables and waved, then explained how happy seeing them every day made me, and I handed them the gift card.

Some of them were completely confused, because they couldn't hear my nervous, shaky voice from 4 tables away...but even the gentleman closest to me, who heard me loud and clear, was hesitant to take my gift card. I had to insist, twice, before he reached out his hand.

They thanked me, joking that I was now part of their coffee club, and I walked across the street to my car, my whole body shaking because I am NOT good at public speaking. In fact, if my big dream comes true- this book actually selling more than 8 copies, and me getting the opportunity to read a chapter aloud at the Midtown Scholar in PA (it's a very specific dream)- I probably won't even be able to get through a paragraph before my throat goes dry and my shaky hands drop the book.

But for now only my kids, my husband and my dog have heard this so let's not get too ahead of ourselves.

So anyway, coffee gift card, shaking, moving on with my life.

The following week, on Tuesday, I waved to the coffee club on my way into the coffee shop and they hesitantly waved back. I was certain that I had creeped them out and went from warm and fuzzy to humiliated in 2 seconds flat. But when I came out with my "check all the boxes on the cup" latte and crossed the street, the mumbling started.

"Are you sure it's her?"

"Yes, it's her, let's go!"

"THANK YOU!"

And here we are, back to the key fumbling.

I looked across the street and saw every one of them waving and smiling, and yelling across the busy intersection, "Thank you so much for what you did! You made our whole day! We really appreciated it! You are so nice! Have a great day!"

Did I do this to make myself feel great? No. I did it make them happy. But did a ringing chorus of thanks across a busy street on a rainy morning make my whole freaking week? Of course it did!

And the following day, when I walked into the coffee shop (after the coffee club and I waved and smiled to each other, as they were now sure that the tall, frizzy-haired redhead they kept seeing was in fact the same one who had bought their coffee), ordered my regular, and handed over my Amex....the shop owner waved her hand at me.

"Nope, it's on them this morning."

And she pointed to my new friends outside.

I ran outside to tell them how much their gesture meant to me, but was stopped short by them telling me how much my gesture had meant to them. We talked for a bit, I was late for work, my coffee was cold...and it was the nicest morning I've had in a really long time.

A simple act of seeing a group of retired friends sharing coffee in the morning led to eight people having hearts full of gratitude and the urge help even more. Everyone went home fuzzy and warm. Everyone won.

And if you want to take the Awwww level to 11- that was the same day that, while the barista whirred the milk for my allergy-friendly fix, I noticed the small giving tree, overloaded with tags, leaning against a window by the straws and napkins. Maybe it was the amount of happy that was bouncing around inside me- maybe I would have done it anyway. I don't know. But I pulled 2 tags, then pulled 2 more the next week, then asked my Facebook friends if anyone wanted to help me out to pull one more.

Three weeks later, I've raised over $4000 from donors across the country; I've shopped for 103 children in need; I've spoken with a local newspaper, who posted the story and inspired others to find more giving trees; and Pat and I are looking into setting up a nonprofit to empty giving trees all year long.

All because of a cup of coffee.

So is there such a thing as a selfless gesture? I'm really not sure. Does it matter? Pretty sure it doesn't.

If someone makes you happy, tell them. It may inspire them to make someone else's day brighter.

If you like someone's scarf, shoes, mohawk or nose ring, compliment them! More than likely, they'll carry that with them for longer than you think. And the happiness bouncing around inside them might lead to things you could have never imagined.

So I say bring on the selfish good deeds!

Just take a lesson from Phoebe and don't place any bets or go looking for a wasp with a trigger butt.

CHAPTER 11

Lights

As is every mother's tagline (especially on class picture day, birthdays, and first/last days of school), "My baby isn't a baby anymore!"

And never has that rung truer for me than it has during this year.

2020 has snatched a lot from me- my social life; my sleep; my big, loud, joyous family holidays; my Sunday afternoon visits with my parents; and most recently, my ability to cross over state lines without quarantining- to name a few. But perhaps the biggest kick in the teeth I've received from the vindictive little donkey that is this year, is that it took away my little boy, and tossed some sort of adolescent/pre-teen precursor at me.

Sometime in April, I finally caved in and let Vince dip a toe into the rabbit hole that is Fortnite, for no other reason than it was virtually the only way for him to connect with his friends during lockdown. And from that moment on, it's been a blur. Hours of ornate Lego masterpieces have been forgotten in lieu of "parties" and "victory royales." Trips to Game Stop for a treasured, rare pack of Pokémon cards have been tossed aside for digital V-buck uploads to buy "skins."

Begging for the newest book in a series has been replaced by begging for a Samsung Galaxy S20.

"Can we cuddle?" has been slapped in the face by, "Can I rake some leaves to earn more screen time?"

But maybe the worst of it- the most painful part of watching him turn from my squishy, clingy little Vinny Bear into someone who would rather be lost in internet space- is losing the drives.

When I was Vince's age, my absolute favorite thing to do was take a ride with my dad. He would come home from a long, grueling day of coaxing cars and trucks back to life, his hands full of cuts and his clothes full of grease, but his eyes still full of sparkle. He'd clean up, sit at the dinner table, and ask all of us about our days while we ate our meal. Then, if I was lucky, he'd wink at me conspiratorially and ask, "Wanna go for a ride?"

I lived for those nights.

Sometimes we stopped at McDonald's for a Happy Meal (shhh, don't tell my mother). Sometimes we'd stop for gas. But most nights, we just got in the car and went wherever Route 80 took us.

It might sound weird, but even though it was 30 years ago, I can still hear the vinyl seats squeaking as I shimmied into his massive 1977 Thunderbird (or as my mother not-so-lovingly referred to it, The Land Yacht). I remember gently pushing the boxes of Marlboros and Freedent gum into the middle of the bench seat between us. He'd slide out a piece of gum with one hand and tune the radio to the oldies station with the other, and we'd be off.

Most nights I rolled the window down (literally, with a crank- 1977, people) just enough to take in the cold night air. It was usually a heady mix of NJ highway, peppermint-flavored gum, and the little tree bobbing around on the rearview mirror. For me, it was the scent of tranquility. Make a candle out of that today and I'd be your best customer.

We rarely spoke- just drove, sometimes for a few hours, listening to Brown-Eyed Girl and Stairway to Heaven and everything in between. I would press my cheek into that cool vinyl headrest, stare out the window, and watch as the sky turned from blue to pink to black. I watched the houses grow farther and farther apart and eventually be replaced by tall, wide evergreens as we ventured further and further west. It was so calming and mesmerizing.

In that car, I learned how to be still. On those nights, without even realizing it, I learned mindfulness, gratitude and meditation. And during those long, tranquil drives, I bonded with my dad. We understood each other so well that neither of us needed to speak. Sometimes we'd hum along with the radio. Sometimes he'd ask if I was hungry, or if I was warm or cool enough. Sometimes I'd ask about all the cars he fixed that day. But mostly, we just drove.

And of all the memories I have of my childhood- the holidays, the birthdays, the vacations- those drives are the most vivid, and the ones that bring me the most contentment.

I'm not sure when we last took a drive. It was probably years ago. Dad has since retired; he has acute stage COPD (thanks to the Marlboros), and after several failed attempts at a double-knee replacement (thanks to spending 4 decades underneath those cars), he is currently in a wheelchair. I miss those nights so much that sometimes it actually hurts to think about them. But I'm so grateful to have had them- to have had a childhood full of that serenity and peace. To have had our time. Our drives.

That's probably why I must have looked like Vince had just pierced me in the eye with a toothpick when he responded to my offer to drive around looking at Christmas lights with, "Um…actually, would it be ok if we just go home so I can play Big Brain?"

I had just sat in my freezing cold Kia for half an hour during his karate practice (well, I did turn the seat warmers on a few times…cars have come a long way since 1977), and I was looking forward to stopping for some hot chocolate and driving around aimlessly, looking for houses that broke the rules and (gasp!) decked themselves out for Christmas a full 3 days before Thanksgiving.

He knew this. We've been taking drives and listening to music for years. Probably since he was a toddler. It's our favorite time together (besides bedtime Harry Potter, of course). He regularly asks to run errands with me just so we can drive around afterward and belt out whatever music we're loving at the moment. Sometimes we stop for hot chocolate. I always ask if he's warm or cool enough.

But mostly, we just drive.

And he wanted to skip that for some game on his

tablet that involves incessant tapping to earn coins that aren't really worth anything but make your character's head bigger.

No really.

I could see that he felt guilty about not wanting to go with me, so I immediately responded, "Sure! No problem- there probably won't be that many houses decorated anyway. It's not even Thanksgiving. I'll take you home."

"Mommy...I'm sorry I'm growing up so fast and that I'm not your baby anymore. I know it's hard for you."

Did I mention my 8-year-old is really a 4ft-tall spiritual guru with an unruly red mop of hair and a slight overnight drooling problem?

"Bud, no. I get it. It's your job to grow up! You can't be a baby forever. It's just, it's happening so fast and I'm trying to hold onto our time together as much as possible. But we can go home so you can play your game."

"Are you sure? I'm sorry, Mommy."

"Dude, don't ever be sorry for growing up. That's your job."

"Are you sure?"

"I'm very sure."

But I took the long way home anyway.

I drove past house after house, smiling at the twinkling lights without saying a word. I knew he just wanted to get home. I wasn't going to try to force quality time on the poor kid.

But as we passed the house on Main Street, the one with the rainbow-colored rope lights in the maple tree- the one that had been one of his favorites for three years- I stole a glance into the back seat and saw his head glued to the microfiber headrest, his eyes wide, and his mouth slightly ajar with the same wonder it had displayed when he was 5 years old.

And I knew in that moment that our drives weren't over yet.

I pulled into the driveway and watched my not-so-little boy hop out of the car, certain he was headed for his tablet. But instead, he watched a cartoon with his sister, brushed his teeth...and asked me to cuddle and read another chapter of Harry Potter.

I, of course, tripped over myself to get to the book.

I admit that before I had kids, whenever parents would complain that their little ones were "growing too fast" it always confused me. I mean, isn't that the goal? Isn't that what we want them to do?

I mean…yes and no.

Grow, absolutely! But also stay small, chubby and giggly. And tap me on the shoulder for warm milk and a cuddle at 2am because you had a bad dream. And wear dinosaur socks. And pronounce strawberry yogurt "strowbelly yo-yuck" until you're 35.

It's not much to ask, really.

But, as I write this and I'm really thinking about it, there is something really cool about them getting older.

For my dad and me, over the years our long, tranquil drives evolved into long, deep conversations about life, usually on the couch after the rest of the house had fallen asleep. When I was in college, and he knew I was really interested in one of my psychology classes, he sat up one night and read my ENTIRE textbook so he could chat with me about it throughout the semester. After I moved into my first apartment, he still called me every time there was a light rain, to remind me to drive carefully because, "light rain brings out the oils in the road, and the idiots."

And one night, when I was 27 years old and had just walked out of an awful job that was supposed to be my fast track to a brilliant career (that I didn't want), I didn't go home to my husband. I showed up at my parent's doorstep, and drove my dad down the shore to eat pizza and Kohr's vanilla orange swirl with sprinkles, and play skeeball and air hockey. We walked up and down that boardwalk and talked about life. I watched the waves crash against the sand and promised him that I knew I'd made the right decision, and that I'd be ok. And he looked at me and replied, "Oh, I know you will be. You're going to be fine."

And hearing him say it, I knew it must be true.

And, spoiler alert- I was.

So yes, they grow up. Really goddamn fast. But I guess in some ways they'll always be your babies.

About a paragraph into this chapter, Vince quietly padded out of his room to tell me a funny story that just couldn't wait until morning, and to ask me to tuck him in again, and give him one extra hug and kiss.

Maybe he's growing up too fast for my liking. Maybe electronics and friends and that weird brain game will eventually replace hot cocoa and Legos.

But I'm pretty sure, even though it will evolve, and maybe he'll be in the driver's seat eventually (God help me), if I play my cards right...I'll always have my baby.

CHAPTER 12

Knowing

"I'm just tired."

I looked into Pat's face and I knew he wasn't tired.

He was TIRED.

It's that time of year. A time filled with festive decorations, chirpy songs about snowmen, menus full of chestnuts and cranberries, and entire birds stuffed with rosemary and sage and hopes and dreams and nostalgia.

But not if you suffer from debilitating depression.

Because if you suffer from debilitating depression, like my husband, the holidays are not a time for twinkling lights and Mariah Carey belting out her holiday wishes in a velour Santa suit.

They're about memories.

Memories of your father, in a drunken rage, hurling

the tabletop tree, the only one your mother could afford, out the living room window- ornaments and all.

Memories of waking up at 6am on Christmas morning, opening your gifts as quickly as possible and then locking yourself in your room before he woke up in a rage and smashed everything.

Memories of grabbing the food your mom had cooked after a 12-hour shift, straight from the pots on the stove, and eating on your bed with the door locked so you could finish a meal without him pushing you up against a wall and wrapping his fist around your throat, to hold you in place while he screamed obscenities into your face.

Memories you don't want, but can't forget.

When we began our friendship during sophomore year of high school, I knew Pat had endured a rough childhood. I didn't know the extent of it, but I knew enough to be aware that my mother's friends had warned her to be "careful" because although he was a "very sweet boy," he came from a "rough family." They didn't want me getting mixed up with that.

Well, I did.

A year later, when we started dating in November, I

immediately invited him to my family's Christmas Eve dinner. I should mention that my family's Christmas Eve dinner involved about 30 people, including several Sicilian women, who all accosted him, hugged and kissed him, and treated him like they'd known him for years. And then, of course, there was my grandmother, Gracie, who bought me a pair of royal blue, crushed velvet bikini underwear, which she made me open in front of everyone and God, and announced, "Since you have a boyfriend now..." Ensue hysterical laughter and my now-husband's face growing darker than the underwear.

We had been dating 1 month.

The underwear incident was followed by my uncles, who, without words, assured him that if he tried to get anywhere near that underwear he'd go missing.

Side notes- poor bastard didn't see me in my underwear for almost 2 years...and he and my grandmother became better friends than Simon and Garfunkel.

And I'm so, so glad he has those memories, because the next year, when he excused himself to my room after stringing lights on the tree with my dad; broke down and sobbed in my arms; and told me the rest of his memories...I could barely breathe.

Now, over 2 decades later, I'm prepared.

When he told me tonight that he was tired, I knew exactly what he meant. And I centered myself for this year's battle.

Pat has come a long way with holidays- and when I say a long way, I mean a loooong way. He's gone from not even wanting to celebrate, to being the guy that's running to Home Depot the weekend before Thanksgiving because he just needs to find the perfect icicle lights for the lilac tree on the side of the house.

He's gone from not even being able to function during the entire months of November and December, to happily scaling the roof to perfectly position the 5-foot spider, making some of the most ornate gingerbread turkeys I've ever seen, and sending me links to Christmas light displays the entire month of December.

He, who never experienced a happy, full-family holiday meal, is one of the best cooks I know. He truly appreciates place settings and holiday napkins. He's the first one to help clear the table after Thanksgiving dinner at my aunt's house. He breathes it all in. It's like he's getting a second chance at childhood.

But that first childhood- that will always be there,

lingering, grabbing him by the throat and throwing him against a wall.

And I always know when it's closing in.

His temper becomes short. His eyes grow cloudy. His energy level drops like the temperatures in January.

The dog is taking too long to pee outside. The kids are chewing too loudly. My voice is condescending. His energy is zapped.

He insists he's fine. I insist he isn't. He insists more loudly. But he may as well have half a dozen bright red flags waving frantically over his head.

This is a dance we do every single year. Often by the middle of December we've had at least one blow out, I've almost willed myself to take the kids and leave, and he has written me a letter that I could read with my eyes closed- he knows I don't deserve this, and he probably won't ever get better, and he warned me in the beginning that he was who he was, and I should go find someone who deserves me.

But that's the thing.

The person he is- is AMAZING, and I have no idea how I got so lucky to deserve him.

The person he is- lived through a childhood so traumatic that I can't even fathom getting through a month of it, let alone eighteen years.

The person he is, rose above his circumstances to push himself through college, build a successful career, find and nurture love, buy a comfortable home, and start a family.

The person he is, went from eating cold food out of the pot on the stove at 8 o'clock at night as a child, to whipping up incredible meals after working a full day, and sitting at the dining room table enjoying them with a wife and two kids who absolutely adore him.

Pat lives to make sure the people he loves are comfy and cozy.

He has a warm towel, a hot shower and a glass of red waiting if he even hears a hint of "I had a day" in one of my text messages.

He packs the kids' lunches with extra snacks and remembers which one of them prefers broccoli and which would rather have green beans.

He constantly smiles at, admires and, if the kids are distracted, playfully grabs every single part of my body that he knows the years have made me feel less than sexy about.

He is the best at soothing boo-boos, helping with art projects, and explaining the finer parts of the grill and the smoker to Vince "eager-to-be-just-like-dad" Vonk.

He sleeps on the floor with the dog when she's sick. When my adrenal disorder flares, he sends me to bed and brings me small, balanced meals every 2 hours until my body resets itself.

When he hugs, he envelopes you into his big, strong arms until you aren't sure where he ends and where you begin, and you no longer care, and you never want to leave.

But when his eyes go dark- they go pitch black.

Suddenly nothing anyone says is right. The way we sit in our chairs irritates him. We're too loud. We don't say hello fast enough when he walks through the door. He's too tired for game night. His back hurts too much to toss the ball around in the back-yard. His head is pounding too much to focus on movie night.

On the worst nights he eats in silence, throws his

dishes in the sink and goes to bed without so much as a goodnight.

We all know- even Grace, at the ripe old age of five.

"Daddy's sad. It's that time of year when he remembers how bad stuff used to be. We need to be extra nice."

Is it a perfect life? No. Do we wish our kids had no idea that he suffers from these demons? Of course. But it's a life that was hard-won, and it's a life that's worth fighting for.

So I stay and I fight, because I know. I know who he is, and where he came from, and how long and hard he worked to crawl from the rubble of the hand he was dealt, to where he is today.

I know. So every year, when he gets thrown against the wall by the throat, I fight alongside him. Because I'll be damned if that childhood creeps back up and strips him of the happy life he created. The happy life he doesn't believe he deserves.

He needs to constantly be reminded that he is NOT the hand he was dealt. He is the person who threw the entire deck of cards in the trash, set it on fire, and created a life so full of love and compassion that even his therapist can't understand how he triumphed over his circumstances.

He is whole. And he is worthy of love. And he is NOT his depression. And, not for nothing, but if he is patient enough to deal with his depression and my crippling anxiety, well, then he's also a candidate for sainthood.

So tonight, when he said he was tired, I knew. It's going to be a long couple of months. It's going to be walking on eggshells and taking deep breaths and giving extra love, and sometimes losing my temper when I should be helping him hold his.

It's not perfect.

But it's worth it.

The holidays aren't exactly magical and carefree for everyone. But every year I watch this man, who I fell in love with before I should have even known what love was, overcome his memories to create much better ones- with lots of ornate gingerbread- for his own kids. And I know I'm probably one of the luckiest people on the planet to get to fight alongside him.

I just know.

CHAPTER 13

Butt Cheeks

Well...that was a bit heavy. Let's switch it up a bit and talk about the most popular subject in my house.

Butt cheeks.

As I'm sitting at my dining room table trying to figure out how to begin, Grace just bounced past me with a cough drop ("I'm fine, it just looked like something I wanted to try"), and I asked her, "What do you think of a chapter about butt cheeks?"

"Definitely!" she replied, popping a honey echinacea in her mouth, vibrating over the couch to watch Bluey, and calling over her shoulder, "I cannot wait to hear the chapter about butt cheeks!!"

Side note: my mother could not WAIT for my daughter to be born.

"Finally, a little princess! A sweet, beautiful little princess."

Sorry Grandma.

While my poor mother spent my entire pregnancy dreaming up an Aurora or a Belle, I birthed Vanellope Von Schweetz.

Grace lives in her own world. She dances through the house until she literally hits a wall, and then theatrically sinks to the ground and howls as though she's been attacked by the wolves in Beauty in the Beast.

She would wear the same outfit 17 days in a row if I let her and, more than once, she has sobbed uncontrollably at the injustice of having to change her underwear "every single day!"

She starts pulling her pants down before she gets to the bathroom; pees with the door open; and never, ever flushes.

Like, ever.

I have nightmares about the number of times I've awoken in the morning, shuffled into my bathroom and found a day-old Mr. Hanky staring up at me.

She doesn't brush her teeth unless coerced. Then she hunts for chocolate.

Ask her if she's washed her hands and she'll reply, "Of course!" Add, "with soap and water?" and you'll see her ball her little fists, turn on her princess heels, and storm back into the bathroom fuming, "Ugh why??!!!!"

This girl will dig for, locate and eat a booger in front of a (horrified) room full of people and then go on her merry way.

If you cuddle her, or allow her to sit on your lap for longer than 3.2 seconds, you're getting farted on. And she will give you a play-by-play.

And then, 9 times out of 10, you will black out.

I've seen her put her brother in a choke hold for fun. I've also had daycare teachers tell me about her punching another kid in the face for messing with her brother.

If Grace is happy, you will know. She will put on every skirt she owns, cake her face with her Frozen II makeup pallet, throw on a cape and a pair of my heels (I'm just glad someone is using them), and sing an entire conversation while she twirls like a top across the house.

If Grace is unhappy- find shelter. The skirts come off, the voice goes from a tinkle to a growl, doors get slammed, floors get stomped...I've actually had to pry her fingers off the front door because she had "had enough of this life" and was "running away forever and ever!!!!"

And when she's not being Te Fiti or Te Ka, she's an unwitting comedian.

If I'm looking for a parking space and she finds one, she yells gleefully, "There! There's a crack between those two cars! Pull into the crack!"

She refers to the space behind her knees as her leg-pits.

The other night I watched as she carefully placed her Moe's burrito on the table, lowered her face onto it, and looked up with cheeks as full as a chipmunk and the most innocently gleeful expression in her eyes as black beans slowly escaped from her lips.

She calls from the shower, "Don't worry, I washed my pagina so I don't get an ouchie in it like you did!" (that's the first and last time she comes with me when I see the dr. for a UTI...)

Grace is as unhinged and free-spirited as they

come- and, disclaimer, I would not want her ANY other way.

Grace is also obsessed with butt cheeks.

She has dubbed Covid, "The stupid butt cheek virus," and it was so catchy that my entire family now uses it in conversation with (often-confused) friends and coworkers.

If you ask what she wants to eat, you're going to get one of two answers:
1. Pizza
2. Butt cheeks

After a long car ride, she will announce to any and all passersby, while rubbing her ass vigorously, "Whoa! My butt cheeks are killin' me from sitting in that booster seat!"

At a nice restaurant, she will get up and quietly explain, "Sorry, just gotta scratch my butt cheeks."

Some of her favorite conversation starters?

"That looks like a butt cheek!"

"Listen to my butt cheeks!"

"Look at my butt cheeks!"

Thankfully, that last one has never happened in public. Oh no wait...I'm wrong.

Last weekend, at a public rest stop, I realized the lock on the stall was broken and told Grace we had to find a new one. So she strolled out of said stall and began walking to another one with her pants still around her ankles. "It's fine, Mommy, we have the whole bathroom to ourselves. This is so nice!"

But that's the only time, thank God.

Oh no...wait.

A few weekends ago, Pat was stringing icicle lights on our lilac tree (yes, the ones he ran to Home Depot to find before Thanksgiving) and I had just snuck outside to make sure he hadn't fallen over the retaining wall. We were discussing icicle positioning when we heard a chirpy voice behind us declare, "Those look so pretty!"

I turned to find Grace admiring her father's handiwork, a serene, sweet smile on her face...and no clothing, besides an ill-fitting toddler towel, on her dripping wet, fresh-out-the-bath body.

Pat later told me, "I had no idea why you screamed until I looked past you and there they were- two butt cheeks."

If Disney ever needs a fresh idea, I may be able to market her as Princess Butt Cheek.

But as soon as you feel like you've been all butt-cheeked out, Princess Butt Cheek does a 180 on you.

Every time I'm on the verge of a "working from home while keeping up with 3rd grade and kindergarten OH MY GOD what is in Marty's mouth now?!" meltdown, I feel the littlest arms wrapping around my waist, look down to find the sweetest eyes looking up at me, and hear the gentlest voice whisper, "You looked like you needed a stress hug."

Every time I'm about to cry during a movie, I feel a little hand slipping into mine and giving it a squeeze.

When Princess Butt Cheek has a nightmare, I often find her standing quietly next to my side of the bed, eyes full of yet-to-spill tears, waiting for me to wake up and silently scoop her into my bed and let her hide from the world in the safety of her mama's arms.

She comments on people's beauty in an ethereal way while walking down the street, and tells us how grateful she is for her family when asked her favorite flavor of ice cream.

So Grace isn't the princess my mother dreamed of

while I vomited my way through those nine long, painful months.

She's her own kind of princess. A raw, real, messy, feisty, emotional, kick-ass, fashion-forward, sing-songy and swift-punching force to be reckoned with.

She's our Princess Butt Cheek.

And she's pretty perfect if you ask me.

CHAPTER 14

Tornadoes

I just watched my 3rd grader nail his virtual presentation on tornadoes. We worked tirelessly on that presentation for an entire week. I, the old lady, showed him how to use literary resources. He, the virtual school guru, showed me shortcuts for inserting pictures into Google Classroom. I sat on his bed with a cup of tea while he read and reread his notes on the Pine/Purvis/Amite storm of 1908 until he could pronounce all the words. He munched on sunflower seeds and gazed at me in awe while I swiftly typed the URL links in his resources page (not bad for an old lady, huh?).

I love research projects- they're like a puzzle that needs to be put together; a riddle that needs to be solved; and an opportunity to learn more about any given subject.

My son detests them.

I have to say, for a kid who spends hours watching the Smithsonian Channel and researching obscure shark tooth facts in his free time, Vince regards research projects with far too much horror. The way his face contorted as he read the instructions, you'd have thought the assignment was to eat a bowl of live poisonous insects.

As we read the instructions, I could see the fear vibrating from his massive orange curls, through his skinny knees and into his new "had to have them" neon green sneakers.

So I asked if he needed help.

"No I'm good."

He's an awful liar…still, I waited a few days.

"How's it going?"

"It's fine. Mrs. Shears is giving us time in class to work on it."

A few days later…

"Is it done?"

"Mrs. Shears is giving us an extra week so it's fine."

"So…how far are you?"

"I did two slides so far."

"Can I see them?"

"Well-"

Oh boy.

"Let me see them."

As any parent reading this may have guessed, the first slide was his name and the second slide was a list of storms from which to choose.

So after a week and a half, my son had written his name and circled the word "Tornadoes."

I looked from the second page to him. He knew what was coming.

"VINCENT!"

And that, Dear Reader, is how I learned all I know about tornadoes.

Here's the thing about Vince- he feels like he needs to take things on all at once (wherever could he have gotten that from?!). The night he received his green belt in karate a few months ago, I cheered and hugged him, and he...teared up in the car.

"If I hadn't taken that month off over the lockdown, I would've had a high green by now. And if I had listened to you and started when I was 4 instead of

6, I'd probably be almost at a black belt. I'm so far behind!"

When we ask him to clean his room, he spirals into a full-fledged panic attack. We have to sit with him and show him how to split it into tiny portions to get him to stop hyperventilating enough to fold his pants and fluff his pillows.

As my husband says whenever I start to spiral (which, honestly, is so often that I'm surprised my body hasn't formed into the shape of rotini), "Cath, you're 17 steps ahead of yourself. One step at a time."

So, when I saw my mini-rotini beginning to spin in front of me as I held his barely-begun project, I knew exactly what to say.

"Vince, how many slides is the project?"

"I'm not sure. I think about 37. At least 37."

I counted- 15. Not quite 37.

"Vince, there are 15. But you're 14 steps ahead of yourself. There's one."

The fear on his face mingled with a concern that I was worse at math than he previously thought.

"What?"

"There's one slide. And when that's done there will be one more. And then another one. And there will be one at a time until you've done them all. You can't do 15 at once- but you can do one."

And so we did.

As he researched one slide after another, I watched Vince's apprehension turn into interest, and then morph into excitement. He looked for more information even after he had answered the question. He searched for the best possible picture on each slide to pair with his new tornado expertise. He asked questions, told jokes, and was genuinely interested in everything he found.

Once the project was done I sat on his bed and listened to his practice presentations. Each time he read through it, his confidence grew. This morning he bounced out of bed and reminded me, "Today is presentatiooonnn dayyy!"

Pretty far cry from the kid who had taken a week to write his name on Slide #1, no?

So here we were- the big moment. Gracie and I sat on his bed to give him some reassurance as he took the Google Meet stage. We took a deep breath, held hands, and waited.

And he NAILED it.

Every word, every fact, every statistic. He read smoothly, clicked the slides when he was supposed to- the kid didn't miss a beat.

I couldn't even give a 30-second speech at my cousin's wedding without shaking so violently that I literally almost choked, and he just sat in front of a computer screen with 20 kids staring at him from Brady Bunch-esque boxes and didn't flinch.

I guess he's a lot less rotini than his mama (thank goodness).

When he finished, he looked back at me and smiled. He was practically glowing. I was as proud as if he had just given a Nobel Prize acceptance speech. When his meet ended he threw himself into my arms and his sister launched herself at him like a little cannon and exclaimed, "I'm so proud of you Vinny!"

Guys- 2020 has been horrendous in so many ways, and I'm pretty confident that I speak for everyone with a pulse when I say that we can't wait to put it behind us.

When this storm begins to ebb, there are so many things I won't miss.

I won't miss juggling kindergarten slides, 3rd grade math problems, and work emails while loading the dryer, emptying the dishwasher, and checking on lunch in the oven, like the pandemic version of The Cat in the Hat.

I won't miss soothing Grace at night when she bursts into tears, mourning the preschool journey she never got to finish, or the friends to whom she never got to say goodbye.

I won't miss visiting my parents through the living room window just to see their faces in person for a few minutes.

I won't miss waiting on a designated tape-marking outside Trader Joe's in the rain for 15 minutes every time I need a few groceries.

I certainly won't miss being trapped in a house all day, every day with two children who produce enough gas to power an industrial-sized pickup truck.

But when it's over, and life goes back to its normal level of chaos...I will miss things like this.

I'll miss being able to put aside the laundry and walk away from the work laptop for half an hour to listen to my son teach me about Tornado Alley.

I'll miss being home to help my daughter play math games and dance to the morning meet's "goodbye song" in the living room every day.

I'll miss being home in time for dinner, and eating lunch at the dining room table with the kids across from me and the dog snoring at my feet, instead of tossing lunch boxes in their bags as we run out the door (probably late, again).

I'll miss having a live look at the smiles of pride and accomplishment on their faces when they master a new skill or overcome an academic hurdle.

I'll miss having a front row seat to them every day.

So while Covid can go f-...well, you know....there are parts of 2020 for which I will always be grateful.

Like tornadoes.

Thanks, 2020, for teaching me all about tornadoes.

CHAPTER 15

And to All a Good Night

"**H**appy New Year, Girlfriend!"

"I peed my pants!" ::hysterical sobs::

And that's how we closed out 2020.

While I was pretty content just lying on the couch, middle finger waving at the TV, as the iconic ball dropped like a hammer on this dumpster fire of a year, my kids expected more than that. And that, of course, was my fault.

I had executed a 3-course menu, a dance party and board games for Thanksgiving. Christmas Eve greeted them with an ugly sweater party, more dancing, homemade cookie decorating, craft projects, and a table full of fish and gourmet desserts. Christmas Day overflowed with presents, movies, a 6-layer lasagna and bacon-wrapped smoked chicken. I wasn't going to get away with takeout and lounging on the couch for NYE.

So I did what I've become a whiz at doing this year- I planned a blowout celebration tailored for our isolation bubble of four.

We had party poppers. We had a firepit and outdoor feast by lantern-light on the freezing patio. We had a pile of games and a table stuffed with appetizers and mocktails. We had music. We had noisemakers. We had sparklers and cheap plastic tiaras.

My house looked like that scene from The Grinch where he imagines the Whos dancing around their houses with their jingtinglers and their floofloovers and their great big electro whocardio flooks.

We didn't have any of those, per say (although I'm sure if I spelled them correctly I could've found them on Amazon)- but we did have Grace.

She emerged from her post-dinner bath in her favorite construction pajamas, slid a pink tiara over her wild curls, tossed a strand of gold beads around her neck, and went to work turning our dining room into a kids' VIP lounge.

She carefully strung streamers onto my grandmother's antique hutch. She proudly organized the toothpicks. She bounced with glee as she assigned a noisemaker to each of us, and then demonstrated how to use them (several times).

All night long, Grace was our NYE cheerleader. She sipped flavored seltzer and berry lemonade mock-tails while she danced around the living room. She curated little toothpick amuse bouchées with red peppers, garlic-stuffed olives and mini-pickles, and presented them to us while she sang, "Snack tiiiime!"

She played the most earnest game of Jenga I've ever seen, squealed every time she slammed down a "+2" card in Uno, and exclaimed, "You win again, girl-friend! You are on FIRE!" every time I bested her in Old Maid.

She laughed so loudly I was pretty sure the neigh-bors could hear her. She heartily complimented every carrot, spring roll and piece of salami that touched her ever-moving lips.

Then she crashed ten minutes before midnight, passed out on Pat's chest, and drooled on his shirt while we clinked our glasses and exclaimed, "Happy New Year!" over her kid-drunk, slumped-over body.

She never woke up as I carried her into bed, which is shocking because the fart she unleashed on my arm was powerful enough to register on the Richter

Scale. We do have evidence that she stumbled into the bathroom sometime in the wee hours and got into a fight with a toilet paper roll. Then she snored soundly until 10:30 this morning, when she and her impressive bed head appeared in her bedroom doorway, looking thoroughly disheveled, confused, and…soggy.

"Happy New Year, girlfriend!" I attempted.

She immediately burst into tears.

"I peed my pants!"

Pat got the floor cleaner, I got the bubble bath and, through tear-inducing laughter, we assured her it was ok. Everyone parties too hard sometimes. Once she was immersed in organic gingerbread-scented bubbles, she regained her clarity enough to smile serenely at me and declare that she'd had "the best time ever," at our party the night before.

She's now sitting on my couch, hoodie pulled up to her eyes, chin-to-feet under a blanket, sipping milk and watching cartoons.

College is going to be fun with this one.

But seeing her grinning through her beard of bubbles, so happy and content in her post-pee bath, gave me pause.

Last night was, dare I say it, a pretty damn good time.

Grace grabbed the last day of what was in so, so many ways, an absolutely despicable year, and molded it into something amazing.

The same way she did when she carefully thumbed through the clothing racks in Target and chose all of our sweaters for Christmas Eve.

The same way she did when she quietly snuggled up to each of us in turn during our Christmas Day movie marathon.

The same way she did when she snuck into Vince's room at 9pm last night, where he'd been passed out since 7:30 (frozen patio bbq did him in), coaxed him awake, and brought him pickles on the couch ("they're his favorite") until he perked up and joined her on the floor for Jenga.

Why?

"He can't miss this, Mommy. This is going to be the greatest night ever."

Kind of like how our Thanksgiving dinner was, "The best meal I've ever eaten," our Christmas Eve dance party was, "The most fun I've ever had," and our table setting for Christmas Day dinner was, "The prettiest the table has ever been."

The more I sit here and think about it...she wasn't wrong.

We often joke that living with Grace is like raising a feral cat, but in many ways she's really a pixie-like being, flitting around and making everything magical in her own way (just don't piss her off or she morphs from Tinkerbell to Maleficent shockingly quickly).

As I'm writing this, she just flitted off the couch and into Vince's room to encourage him as he builds a massive Lego Hogwarts Castle. I can hear her telling him how amazing it looks and how talented he is.

To be honest, I've been pretty convinced that I was the glue that held this shit show together for the past 10 months (I may or may not have actually yelled something to that effect more than once when my three housemates were all acting up at the same time). I think a lot of us feel that way. I've educated my kids; worked remotely; cooked; cleaned; torn apart room after room; created new meals, new activities, and new adventures. I've given hugs and undivided attention when the kids needed to vent their frustration and loneliness. I nursed Pat back to health when he contracted Covid, then helped him navigate his way to a new job in the midst of pandemic uncertainty.

So here I was, thinking I had, like so many others this past year, mastered a Zen-like level of multi-tasking and mommy magic.

But then the holidays rolled around, and all of my magic went dim.

I'm tired. I'm lonely. I'm frustrated.

As Thanksgiving approached, I longed to walk through the front door of Aunt Cathy's living room, be greeted with a hug and the intoxicating aroma of turkey, and let my eyes take in the magic of her cozy candlelit living room and perfectly-set tables in the dining room.

I wanted to fill my sister Nicky's shot glass with our annual tradition- moonshine- while our entire family filled her with praise for using this year to finally pursue her dreams of attaining that long-desired Psychology degree.

I wanted to pig out on icebox cake with my god-daughter, Merideth, and hear all about her nursing classes at Rutgers. I wanted to listen to my husband, my cousin Charlie, and my Uncle Tony swap work stories over coffee. I wanted to take in Uncle Stu's infectious laugh; listen to Uncle Mike play his guitar; and giggle at the table with Aunt Denise. I wanted to hear Aunt Roxanne and my mother tell stories of holidays past, laughing so hard the tears would eventually spill into their dessert plates. I wanted to peek into the living room and see my kids playing with their cousins, Donnie & Mikayla, while my dad took his post-turkey nap on the couch.

I'd get none of it this year. All I got was an endless loop of doom.

"What if this never ends? What if it claims one of us? Or more than one? What if I never experience that scene again?"

So why bother?

While we're at it, why in God's name would I even try to replicate Christmas Eve at Renee and Tina's house? Why try to recreate the intoxication of being surrounded by dozens of cousins and distant cousins and "of course we're cousins!" for hours; having indoor snowball fights; wandering through rooms full of food and laughter; taking candid pictures of cousin Vinny in his Grinch sweater and Ruthann in her plaid pjs; and watching my kids sing Christmas carols at the piano with their cousins Matty & Bren?

How could I ever compete with that?

So why bother?

The "lead with gratitude" mantra that my therapist has spent the last four years instilling in me was slowly replaced by my new, overtired, edgy "who cares, everything sucks" credo.

My glue came apart.

But Grace quietly and unknowingly swooped in and became the glue- the glitter glue, if you will- of a holiday season that I was dreading so immensely that I was on the verge of skipping it altogether.

She reminded me- all of us, really- that the magic is where you are. Sometimes it's created for you. Sometimes you have to work for it.

This year I got to create it, with the help of a very sage five-year-old.

This year's holidays were magical on a completely different level. And while I eagerly await the holiday season that involves Aunt Cathy's turkey, Renee's homemade sushi, and Fran & Ryan's warm, inviting NYE get-together, complete with allergy-friendly snacks and homemade booze...and of course one or two vegan-food and laugh-until-we-cry holiday dates with my bonus family- I don't think I will ever forget the kind of joy I experienced in my little house, with my little isolation bubble of 4, these past few months.

Grace is sitting next to me right now, twirling some confetti and pondering, "I think maybe we got a little too crazy with the streamers last night."

No, Girlfriend.
It was just right.

CHAPTER 16

I Hate When My Mother Is Right

But she **was.**

That crazy woman was right.

I did write a book.

She sighed and laughed and awwwed while I read her the last chapter over the phone last night- just like she does when I read anything to her. Then she said matter-of-factly, "Now go get it published."

"Well, I still need to edit each chapter, figure out what to do with a cover, and research how to sell it on Amazon," I explained.

"Ok so do it. Start researching."

Here's the thing about my mother- there are two of her. It's the Tale of Two Rosalies.

There's the woman who swore she didn't know what the Check Engine light in her minivan looked like. She just knew "something was blinking." She's been married to a mechanic for forty years.

There's the woman who tried to tell me my writing style reminds her of an author she used to love reading, "Merma Bommeck....Berma Mombeck.... Berm...uuuggghhh...Er....Ma....Bom....Beck. There. Merma Ombeck. Ugh!" (And for the record, that's her opinion, not mine. She's a mom; it's her job to compare her children to famous people).

There's the woman who timidly hides containers of spare ribs and pork lo mein when I come over so I won't lecture her about her sodium and saturated fat intake.

There's the woman who becomes a welcome mat when she babysits- never raises her voice, feeds them more crap in 3 hours than I'd allow in a month, and plays the part of the giggly, doting grandma to a T.

And then there's Other Rosalie.

That woman saw me shuffling from foot to foot in her bedroom doorway after my first date with Pat, put down her book and smiled at me as I blurted out, "I think I'm going to marry him." I expected some sort of lecture- after all, I was only 16 years old. What the hell would I know about love?

But she didn't lecture. Instead, she quietly replied, "I believe you. I knew the moment I met your father that he was the one. We were engaged six weeks after we met. Everyone told us we were crazy; my priest even refused to marry us. And here we are. So if you know he's the one, then I know he's your 'one' too."

That woman told me without hesitation that I needed to put my fears aside and move ahead with buying my house, because she had dreams of her own when she was my age and she let her fear take them from her.

"I was going to be a caterer. I was going to be a beautician. I dreamed of owning a home with a wrap-around porch. But I was scared, so I let them all go. Don't do that to yourself, Cathy. Go buy that house."

And that woman is the woman who has told me, time after time, "This isn't your path, Cathy. Write the book. That's your path." Through every step of the career that didn't fulfill me. Through the last eight years of the comfortable job with the coworkers that have become like family, she still quietly reminds me, "It's a great place to be, Cathy, but it isn't your path. Write the book."

Last night, when I had spoken the last few words of the last chapter, that woman said, "I've been waiting for this your whole life, Cathy. I knew you could do it. And you did."

I guess I did.

And I did it at the dining room table in the house I had been afraid to buy; while that guy I went on a date with 21 years ago entertained our two children, walked our dog, and placed a hearty lunch next to me so I wouldn't get shaky while I wrote.

So my mom, she's a lot of things.

She's the woman who swore she didn't know that a Belgian waffle with whipped cream, berries and syrup didn't have enough protein to be a real breakfast. She's the woman who used to do Balki Bartokomous' Dance of Joy from the 80's sitcom *Perfect Strangers*, every year on the last day of school. She's the woman who put Christmas tablecloths on our couch one year to make it look more festive.

She's also the woman who spent every day of an entire summer sitting at our kitchen table, feeding me watermelon and playing Yahtzee with me, because watermelon was all I could keep down, and Yahtzee kept my mind too busy to remember how much my 9-year-old body was being ravaged by a mystery infection that none of the doctors could name or cure. Come to think of it, they never did figure it out. Maybe watermelon and repetitive dice games healed me.

As much as it breaks my heart to say it, once pale, sick 9-year-old me turned into healthy, strong-willed 13-year-old me, I spent many years at odds with both of those women. We could barely get through a long lunch without arguing. But the entire time, I missed my dancing, singing, dice-slinging partner.

I'm happy to say we've since learned to let our personalities complement each other, instead of butting heads like two bison protecting their patch of the grasslands. We can chat from lunch into dinner; she's the first person I call whenever I have any kind of news; and I've become the one doing ridiculous dances with my kids, who are increasingly giving me the same look that I used to give her.

I haven't draped tablecloths on my couches yet, but I did use one as a tree skirt.

So I guess what I'm trying to say, Mom, is that I see what you did there. Behind the façade of the woman dancing around the living room with a toilet bowl brush as a microphone (it was unused, I promise), there lies an entirely other Rosalie, patiently steering, coaxing and guiding...while also insisting that chicken smothered in mayo and swiss cheese and draped with a blanket of ham is healthy.

I hate when you're right- and I'm starting to see that you've been right a lot (but I still respectfully disagree about the mayo chicken).

I wrote the book, Mom.

Thank you.